SHAPE YOUR WORLD

Transformational Leadership for Everyday Life

David Timms

Oak Tree Press
Rocklin, California

Library of Congress Cataloging-in-Publication Data

Timms, David.
SHAPE YOUR WORLD: Transformational Leadership for Everyday Life
ISBN-13: 978-1719182942
ISBN-10: 1719182949

1. Leadership. 2. Transformational Leadership.

Printed in the United States of America.

Cover Design by Jonathan Fink

Oak Tree Press
The mighty oak tree, barren in the winter but vibrant in the Spring, stands as a glorious metaphor for human life in the hands of God.

DEDICATION

This book is dedicated to the transformational leaders of IberoAmerican Ministries who serve the people of Chile, Peru, Ecuador and the Middle East with such authenticity, inspiration, empathy, and innovation. Their schools, churches, and community projects help thousands of men, women, and children flourish who might otherwise be lost to poverty, violence, and despair. You can find out more about this remarkable organization at www.iamweb.org.

To that end, all proceeds from this book will support the work of IberoAmerican Ministries.

"If the highest aim of a captain were to preserve his ship, he would leave it in port forever." — Thomas Aquinas

May this book show you a way to not only leave port but discover new lands.

TABLE OF CONTENTS

Foreword

I am biased. No, that is not strong enough. I am addicted. In this case, I hope you will agree that my addiction is life giving! I am addicted to transformation. I am addicted to the power of God to change a life, a family, a community, and a nation. I believe that God longs for us to become more like him and to extend his presence and grace wherever we go.

Robert Kennedy once said, "Some men see things as they are, and ask why. I dream of things that never were, and ask why not." That's how I feel. Similarly, Robert Jarvik (inventor of the artificial heart) has noted that "leaders are those with a poorly developed sense of fear and no concept of the odds stacked against them."

My bias (or addiction!) for transformation long ago led me to the study and practice of leadership. Now, almost four decades later, I have some measure of expertise (at least by Malcolm Gladwell's often referenced "10,000 hours" standard) and lots of experience in leadership. With that background, you should know this:

I LOVE THIS BOOK!

My friend and colleague at William Jessup University, Dr. David Timms, has distilled the rich literature on transformational leadership in this easy to read and highly applicable resource. Read these pages and you will have a clear understanding of leadership, transformation, and how *you* can become more effective in your leadership and relationships. This book bridges the gap between theory and practice in a gloriously wonderful way.

Our society is experiencing tremendous shifts in families, organizations, and communities. At each "pain point", we are crying out for leaders and effective leadership, and I am confident that this book will be a helpful resource to serve you and your network in becoming more effective as a transformational leader. I believe you are called by God to shift the atmosphere wherever you are and wherever you go. Congratulations on getting this book; it will help you transform yourself, your practice of leadership, and shape the world around you.

Dr. John Jackson
President, William Jessup University
June 2018

Preface

Over the years I have read prolifically on leadership, mostly from authors who are *not* faith-based. I often find their materials deeply compelling, insightful, and inspiring. However, my own writing reflects a certain seamlessness between leadership and Christian theology. I have no ulterior motive in doing so, but Christian faith has been core to my identity and calling for nearly fifty years, so it would be disingenuous to suppress it in a work like this. Consequently, I hope that this book reflects the very authenticity and integrity I would encourage in every leader; that you feel the gentle ebb and flow between Jesus and Adam Grant (and many others) that feels so natural to me.

In 2015, William Jessup University established a *School of Christian Leadership* and updated its Mission Statement to read: *"In partnership with the Church, William Jessup University exists to educate transformational leaders for the glory of God."*

What a terrific Mission Statement. It describes who we do it with (the Church), who we do it for (God), and what exactly it is that we do. We educate transformational leaders. But what is transformational leadership? How should we understand it? Even more importantly, how should we apply it to everyday life?

Within the *School of Christian Leadership*, we began to have regular and probing conversations about the deep need for better leadership in society and how we might best define leadership. Several of our faculty had earned doctorates in the field of leadership, and the discussions happened in hallways, classrooms, lunchrooms, and offices.

It was the perfect greenhouse.

I've had leadership responsibilities for nearly four decades, but nothing has captured my imagination like transformational leadership. I wish I had been diving deeply into this as a parent, a pastor, a professor, an elder, and a University administrator long before now. It has been turning everything around. This profoundly simple but life-changing model of leadership has rejuvenated me and given me memorable language for describing what leadership is, and is not. Even more importantly, it has given me concrete steps to take in producing change and building lives. I'm no longer throwing darts blindfolded.

I'm hopeful that this book may help build a small greenhouse for your own leadership development and conversations. Each chapter concludes with some suggested exercises and some space for you to jot down a thought or a question from the chapter which you might take up with a friend. We learn best together!

To that end, I'm grateful for my colleagues, particularly Dr. Dennis Nichols and Dr. Daniel Gluck. They have sharpened my own thinking on leadership, inspired me with their own insights and thoughtfulness, and encouraged me to gather these thoughts together. None of us write or speak in a vacuum. And what you read in the following pages reflects far more collaboration than you might imagine.

Special thanks to Dr. John Jackson, president of William Jessup University, whose own commitment to leadership brought this conversation to the campus with such focus and intensity.

Let me also extend my thanks to the many faculty who serve either full-time or part-time at the University. You provide such valuable leadership on the campus, leading young minds to new places and great heights. So many of you model transformational leadership in so many ways. You are authentic, inspiring, empathetic men and women, and I'm honored to serve alongside you.

Finally, and most importantly, thanks to those students who have come to William Jessup University and accepted the challenge and responsibility to prepare for better leadership in homes, communities, churches, and nations. On the one hand, anyone with the opportunity and resources for private higher education must seriously consider their place in a world marked by poverty, illiteracy, violence, and displacement. Global leadership is not too much to embrace! On the other hand, leadership is a calling of the highest order. May this book encourage you and guide you to produce change and build lives every day.

David Timms, PhD
June 2018

Introduction

"We need leaders not in love with money but in love with justice. Not in love with publicity but in love with humanity. Leaders who can subject their particular egos to the pressing urgencies of the great cause of freedom.... A time like this demands great leaders." – Dr. Martin Luther King, Jr.

Leaders form the front-line of culture.

Would we have the abolition of slavery without William Wilberforce and Abraham Lincoln? Indian independence without Mahatma Ghandi? Women's suffrage without Susan B. Anthony? Civil Rights without Rosa Parks and Martin Luther King, Jr.? The end of South African apartheid without Nelson Mandela? Microsoft without Bill Gates? Apple without Steve Jobs? Saddleback Church without Rick Warren? Berkshire Hathaway without Warren Buffet?

However, while it is easy to point to major (and memorable) leadership figures throughout history, the most personal and impactful day-to-day leadership comes from those in the trenches. The leaders who shape our lives most dramatically are probably the parents who raised us, the teachers who mentored us, the bosses who employed us, and the pastors who guided us.

These people, whose names remain largely unknown beyond our circles, have created our circles. They define and shape our values, our expectations, our choices, and our experiences. Some of their influence in our lives was taught; some was caught.

If you jotted down the names of the ten most influential people in your life, whom would you include? Your list might include one or two recognizable figures, but the majority of your list would probably include names known only by you and a handful of people.

To put it simply, the *real* leaders in our lives are typically not famous historical figures or celebrities, but people with whom we've spent considerable periods of time (or whose books we've read) and whose voices we've given particular authority. We tend to listen to people and follow people whose character and care have touched us in significant ways.

> If you have a place of influence or opportunity in the lives of others, you are a leader.

If *you* have a place of influence and opportunity in the lives of others, whether you stand on large platforms in front of people or sit on a non-profit Board that meets once a month, whether you guide an organization (or part of one) or primarily mentor mothers of pre-schoolers over coffee, you are a leader.

Leadership truly comes in all shapes and sizes. Some people have formal leadership roles marked by titles, responsibilities, and salaries; others have informal roles, mentoring and coaching others behind the scenes. Some leaders have very public profiles; others prefer relative privacy. Some use social media prolifically; others reject it entirely.

But this we can say about true leadership. It's not for the faint-hearted, the ill-prepared, or the spiritually immature.

And by most measures we have a crisis of leadership in our culture.

CRISIS OF LEADERSHIP

Few people would contest the statement that we need more leadership and better leadership at every level. In their best-selling book *Why are We Bad at Picking Good Leaders*, Jeffrey Cohn and Jay Moran cite a 2010 poll in which "almost 70 percent of Americans believe that there is a 'crisis of leadership' in the United States."[1]

Families, churches, businesses, and communities face unprecedented challenges and, for the most part, effective leadership lags far behind those challenges. Those challenges include not only competitive pressures and financial pressures, but also a dramatically changing landscape. The social and workplace fabric of society is undergoing a monumental shift.

In 2018, former U.S. Labor Secretary Robert Reich noted that "The best estimate is about 30 percent of all jobs that people now do will be lost to technology. But most of these will be replaced by new jobs."[2] This in itself poses a particular dilemma. If 30 percent of current jobs are likely to disappear, then we will need leaders for 30 percent new workplace positions than currently exist. The leadership challenge continues to grow.

When it comes to the crisis of leadership, many people bemoan the breakdown of morality in our day, or point their finger at technology as the Damocles' sword threatening to destroy the fabric of society. Others complain about the loss of civility, or become cynical about education. But these changes have happened under our watch.

Newton's Second Law of Thermodynamics reminds us that decline and disorder always happen if energy is not injected into a system. We see this every day. Beds don't make themselves when we get out of them. Dishes don't clean themselves without a little help from us. Our kids' rooms descend into chaos without some serious organizational effort from time to time. Much as we might like those toys to pop themselves back in the box or up on the shelf after playtime, it just doesn't happen. The system needs an injection of energy — usually ours.

> We cannot lead on auto-pilot. Effective leadership demands intentionality, focus, and effort.

Why would we assume that leadership functions any differently? We cannot lead on auto-pilot. Effective leadership demands intentionality, focus, and effort. We cannot simply coast.

Harry S. Truman once noted, "In periods where there is no leadership, society stands still." In reality, however, society doesn't stand still. It never does. Any number of forces will rush to fill a leadership vacuum. It is much truer to say that in periods where we fail to seize a leadership opportunity, someone else will seize it for us or from us.

Some people are shy about stepping into leadership, for fear of failure or disapproval from others. Yet others resist leadership because of its demands. "Too much effort; too much risk," they think. Still others will gladly step up, but only because leadership serves their own needs for affirmation, power, or control. Finally, too many people accept the role of leadership but without any commitment to grow as a leader. All of this adds to the chaos and the crisis.

Leadership indeed demands much of us — courage, effort, energy, consistency, security, and growth, to say the least. This is no small matter.

Think briefly about parenting, for example. The 2011 U.S. census data indicate that in the United States today there are *at least* 13.6 million single parents (83 percent of them are mothers) raising over 21 million children. Leadership in a single-parent family will stretch the best of people. Or consider those families where the parents find their identity in the reputation of their children, and consequently turn their homes into command and control centers. The kids are regimented, structured, organized, and controlled to always reflect well on their parents. But tight boundaries and strict control do not necessarily equate with good leadership. Or ponder the many other homes where parents simply provide food and shelter for their kids until those kids can finally turn 18, move out (or head to college), and look after themselves.

In every instance, we have either the absence of leadership or the abdication of leadership and the outcome is rarely good; broken families, damaged lives, and another loss for the community.

In 1624, the English poet John Donne penned a series of brief devotions. One of those, titled *Meditation 17*, reads in part:

> No man is an island, entire of itself; every man is a piece of the continent, a part of the main. If a clod be washed away by the sea, Europe is the less, as well as if a promontory were, as well as if a manor of thy friend's or

of thine own were: any man's death diminishes me, because I am involved in mankind, and therefore never send to know for whom the bell tolls; it tolls for thee.

Donne captured it well. Much as we might think of ourselves as autonomous and independent, we are inextricably linked to each other and to the world. Whatever choices we make, ultimately affect others—perhaps many others. Like the proverbial flutter of a butterfly's wing on one side of the globe that yields a hurricane on the other side, we should measure leadership in terms of the many ripples it sends out, not just the immediate and noticeable impact.

LEADERSHIP RIPPLES

Even while many of us would identify leadership to be almost at crisis levels, there has been (and is) always hope for formative leadership at all levels. Think about the impact of good *parental* leadership, for example.

Jonathan Edwards (1703-1758) was one of the premier American preachers and theologians of the 18th century. He and his wife Sarah had eleven children, three of whom went on to become luminaries themselves. One son, Jonathan Edwards, Jr., wrote extensively on the abolition of slavery. A daughter, Esther Edwards grew up to become the mother of vice president Aaron Burr, Jr. Meanwhile Pierpont Edwards, another son, served as a delegate in the Continental Congress and as a federal judge.[3] The ripples from one family, where good leadership was exercised and modeled, were far-reaching.

Or consider a humble woman on the other side of the Atlantic Ocean at the same time as Jonathan Edwards.

Susanna Wesley (1669-1742) was the last of twenty-five children in her own family. At age nineteen she married Samuel Wesley, a marriage that would prove troubled and difficult for the next forty-seven years. Together they had nineteen children, nine of whom died as infants. Tragically, at Susanna's death, only eight of her nineteen children were still alive. She had grieved the passing of eleven of them! Among those who lived were John and Charles Wesley. Both men were used powerfully by God to bring revival to Wales and England, and it's been said of their mother:

> Although she never preached a sermon or published a book or founded a church, (she) is known as the Mother of Methodism. Why? Because two of her sons, John Wesley and Charles Wesley, as children consciously or unconsciously will, applied the example and teachings and circumstances of their home life.[4]

Jonathan Edwards and Susanna Wesley modeled transformational leadership in very different spheres (public and domestic), yet they

> *Don't underestimate the potential of your own leadership.*

shaped generations far beyond what either of them could possibly have imagined. They couldn't see into the future, but they deeply influenced the future by leading faithfully where they were. Don't underestimate the potential of your own leadership.

MYTHS ABOUT LEADERSHIP

We've often made assumptions about leadership that do not prove true or, at best, prove only partly true. Before we can examine transformational leadership, we need to air and consider these myths. The first myth of leadership is that leadership is innate or intuitive.

1. *Leadership is innate or intuitive.*
In past generations, particularly with the Great Man Theory of leadership, people commonly concluded that "leaders are born not made."[5] Many folk decided that leadership was mostly about physical and personality traits, which you either had or didn't have. People believed and taught that social standing and appearance determined leadership capacity and likely success. Interestingly, nothing has really changed. Dan Allender notes:

> A therapist who is considered more attractive will have three times the perceived credibility than the one who is seen as unattractive. A communicator who is more physically attractive will be regarded as more knowledgeable and truthful than an average-looking one even if their presentations are identical.[6]

Anthropologists, sociologists, and psychologists all speak of the natural ascendancy of physically imposing figures. Indeed, research in Malcolm Gladwell's book *Blink* indicates that tall white men are disproportionately represented among CEOs of Fortune 500 companies in America. Gladwell found that "in the U.S. population, about 14.5 percent of all men are six feet or taller. Among CEOs of Fortune 500 companies, that number is 58 percent."[7] Do tall men really make the best leaders? Gladwell concluded:

Most of us, in ways that we are not entirely aware of, automatically associate leadership ability with imposing physical stature. We have a sense of what a leader is supposed to look like, and that stereotype is so powerful that when someone fits it, we simply become blind to other considerations.[8]

While there can be no doubt that height may incline people to look up to us literally and metaphorically, we can easily say that not every six foot tall person is a natural leader. On the other hand, first impressions can make all the difference in terms of either hurdles or opportunities. Sylvia Ann Hewlett, in her powerful book *Executive Presence* discusses the importance of appearance.

> *Research is conclusive that effective leadership is something we learn.*

The most important thing you can do, our qualitative data shows, is to signal fitness and wellness. It's not how much you weigh, but how resilient you seem that enhances or detracts from your executive presence—because leadership is demanding. We tend not to entrust our toughest jobs to people who look like they might keel over from a heart attack.[9]

Initial leadership impressions are often related to physical, biological, or genetic elements. However, recent research is absolutely conclusive that effective leadership (beyond initial impressions) is something that we largely learn. It is more a matter of nurture (what we learn) than nature (what we were born with).

If leadership was innate or intuitive—part of our genetic coding—then it would be much easier (and more successful) than we commonly see. The fact that CEOs and other leaders frequently seek out and pay significant sums of money—often in excess of $300 per hour—for mentors, consultants, advisors, and executive training[10] should be ample evidence that leadership can be learned and needs to be learned, whether we are tall and beautiful or not. Indeed, the rise of peer-mentoring groups like Vistage and its Christian equivalent Converge seems to affirm that leaders seek not only networking but also peer-advising.

Concurrent with the false view that good leadership is innate ("I'm just wired for leadership") is the false assumption that it must therefore also be easy. The second myth of leadership, though rarely stated in these precise terms, assumes that leadership is simple or easy. "People have over-complicated it!"

2. *Leadership is simple and easy.*

Leadership in simple contexts might be simple, but most leadership involves great complexity. It's one thing to lead a group of volunteers to stack chairs at the end of an event. But it's infinitely more complex to lead a church or a team of salespeople over a long period of time.

Most leadership involves the complexity of vision casting, strategic planning, prioritization, conflict management, recruiting and motivating, people skills, task management, and a host of other equally complex elements. Project management often requires a high level of sophistication and expertise.

In short, if leadership was both innate and simple, we'd have successful leaders all around us, and everything would be flowing smoothly and effectively in every sphere of our communities. Has that been your experience? We might also consider a third myth of leadership.

3. Leadership is all about character.

In Christian circles, we have often reduced leadership to matters of character. We assume that the most patient, moral, and ethical people make for the best leaders. This is entirely understandable. In recent decades, we've witnessed a widespread and alarming moral decline in corporate and political America.

Long before the collapse of Enron (2001) and constantly since that time, we've seen ethical failure in churches, workplaces, and homes. At the time of this writing, the United States is undergoing a significant reckoning on the issue of sexual harassment by leaders. Hollywood producers, Washington politicians, mega-church pastors and a host of others are coming under heavy

> *Character alone – even godly character – does not assure or guarantee competent leadership.*

and appropriate fire for their unethical and abusive practices. And Christians might quickly – perhaps too quickly – point to these leadership failures and cry out: "Leadership is all about character." But good character does not ensure good leadership. We have many very fine people in society, Christians and non-Christians alike, whose lives are morally strong, ethically consistent, generous, and thoughtful. Yet, this does not make them leaders.

Godly character matters. But character alone does not assure or guarantee that a person will be competent and effective as a leader.

These false assumptions abound. If leadership was intuitive and easy, we'd be coasting. But it's not; and we're not. If leadership emerged just from fine character, we might be in good shape, but there are a great many fine and moral people who are not strong leaders. There's a subtlety and art to effective leadership.

GET READY; BE READY

Leaders get ready; leaders are ready. Adlai Stevenson once quipped: "It's hard to lead a cavalry charge if you think you look funny on a horse."[11] So what are we doing to become more comfortable in the saddle, to learn the subtleties of horse-riding, and to understand the nuances of horsemanship? Of course, I'm speaking about the saddle of leadership.

> Twenty years of leadership experience has become, for many people, one year of leadership experience repeated twenty times.

Twenty years of leadership experience has become, for many people, one year of leadership experience repeated twenty times. However, leadership in a changing world must be constantly changing and developing. Leaders on auto-pilot are leaders in decline.

In *Rogue Heroes* Ben MacIntyre tells the story of the formation of the British SAS (Special Air Service) in World War II. [12] The SAS would eventually serve as the model for the U.S. Navy Seals and Delta Force as well as Special Forces in other countries around the world.

Lieutenant David Stirling of the Scots Guards originally proposed to British High Command the idea of a small group of commandos who could parachute behind enemy lines, disrupt enemy operations, and quickly slip away; guerrilla warfare. It was a novel idea in World War II.

To prepare, Stirling recruited a small group of men—mostly seasoned soldiers with ice in their veins—and they "got ready." The training regimen was unlike anything that other military personnel had experienced.

To simulate parachute landings in a wind-swept desert (and lacking a plane to make actual drops), Stirling and his men jumped off the back of Jeeps traveling at 35 miles per hour. Broken bones, sprained limbs, cuts, abrasions, and bruises quickly brought the haphazard training practice to an end. But they were "getting ready."

Those first SAS troops studied maps and learned star navigation. In the deserts of North Africa, where sand dunes swept as far as the eye could see, they could not navigate by landmarks...and nobody had GPS.

Then there were the long desert marches to build stamina and endurance. The unit would take minimal water, to condition their bodies to require as little hydration as possible. Later this would save the life of one SAS member, Jack Sillito, who was thought to be lost or captured but trekked 180 miles across the forbidding desert back to the base camp, on his own.

The extraordinary feats of the SAS required extraordinary preparation; learning about explosives, conditioning their bodies for grueling conditions, understanding weaponry, and developing nerves of steel. And the SAS had a profound impact on the Allied war effort.

Transformational leadership today requires no less dedication and preparation. The journey ahead for us (as parents, pastors, teachers, or community leaders) will involve unknown challenges, expansive stretches of desert, and minimal resources at times. What are you doing to not only survive the conditions but to complete the mission *despite* the conditions?

What does it take to get ready and be ready?

Among other things, leaders are readers. When Larry Page, CEO of Google was asked how he learned to run a company, he responded, "I read a lot." In fact, he read three books just on how to name things.[13] Bill Gates once devoured 112 books, articles, or whitepapers during one of his famous "Think Weeks." Mark Cuban (owner of the Dallas Mavericks) reads three hours a day. Mark Zuckerberg (CEO, Facebook) had a personal development plan in 2015 to read a book every two weeks. In fact, author Brad Smart found that A-player executives typically read twenty-four books per year.[14]

Where do these highly successful leaders find the time to read? They make the time. They prioritize their reading because they know that creativity and leadership insight doesn't emerge from thin air. It stands on the shoulders of others.

Stephen Sample, former president of University of Southern California concludes: "To a greater extent than we realize, and to a far greater extent than we would ever care to admit, we are what we read." He goes on to dismiss the value of the daily news and encourage leaders to read (and re-read) the classics of human history.[15]

How do we get ready and be ready as leaders? We read, we learn, and we rehearse.

When God entrusts leadership to us, we have a stewardship responsibility to get ready and be ready. What might you do today and this week to prepare? What might you read, write, practice, or seek advice about? Intentionality is everything. Leaders get ready; leaders are ready.

NOTHING NEW

The idea of leaders taking great steps to prepare for leadership is not new. We see it throughout the Gospels.

Jesus' disciples spent three years getting ready for leadership. He did not come to them and say, "Just do what you already know to do!" Quite the contrary. He required them to leave their jobs, families, and homes and follow him closely for three years, watching and learning new ways— kingdom ways—of leading. Peter's impulsive, self-confident, and dominant ways would need to change. James and John, known as Sons of Thunder, would have to undergo some serious personal transformation.

> *When God entrusts leadership to us, we have a responsibility to get ready and be ready.*

Matthew's inclination (as a tax-collector) to manipulation and exploitation could not continue.

Can you imagine if Jesus had simply resigned himself to these alpha males doing more of what they already knew? It would have scuttled their kingdom leadership in a heartbeat. Instead, they had to leave their livelihoods and neighborhoods, hit the road, try new things, learn new values, and experience transformation in their own lives. They had to *get ready*, so that they would *be ready*.

How much effort and diligence do we pour into our own preparation for leadership? How committed have we been to biblical grounding, kingdom thinking, leadership understanding, and people learning? How much attention do we give to self-knowledge and self-awareness (emotional intelligence)? How willing are we to submit to "painful mentoring"?

The apostle Paul affirmed that "if anyone aspires to an office of leadership, it's a fine thing they desire" (1 Timothy 3:1). It's an even finer thing when they move beyond aspiration to preparation.

This book is part of your preparation for more effective, more thoughtful, and (hopefully) more God-honoring leadership. The core principles of transformational leadership relate as much to building families as building churches or companies. If you're willing to embrace the mantle of leadership, become more than you already are, and do more than you already know to do, I invite you to read on.

CHAPTER SUMMARY

Leadership matters, and it matters at every level of society; politicians, business owners, pastors, and parents. Yet, we face a crisis of leadership—not the lack of people who will lead, but the lack of people who can lead well. We also face a crisis because we've accepted certain myths about leadership, namely, that leadership is intuitive, simple, or primarily about character. Effective leadership is anything *but* these things.

Yet, there's good news. Leadership is more nurture than nature. We *can* learn it, and we *must* learn it. Indeed, readiness for leadership is a core stewardship responsibility for everyone who has the opportunity to influence the lives of others. This readiness for leadership involves reading, learning, and rehearsing. Only then can we become both transformed and transformational.

NOTES

Key thoughts you had while reading this chapter. **Questions** that came up. **Ideas** for personal next steps. **Insights** to discuss with a friend.

Chapter 1

Transformational Leadership

"The leaders who work most effectively, it seems to me, never say 'I.' And that's not because they have trained themselves not to say 'I.' They don't think 'I.' They think 'we'; they think 'team.' They understand their job to be to make the team function. They accept responsibility and don't sidestep it, but 'we' gets the credit. This is what creates trust, what enables you to get the task done." – Peter F. Drucker

What's the magic sauce for successful leadership? Everyone's looking for it, and the field of leadership studies has burgeoned since the 1970s as people have tried to understand and explain the nature of leadership.[16]

Casey Stengel (1890-1975), the Major League Baseball Hall of Famer and New York Mets manager, once noted: "The key to being a good manager is keeping the people who hate me away from those who are still undecided."[17] It's humorous and not bad advice, but it hardly defines good leadership.

In reality, leadership (in every sphere of life) comprises two fundamental elements — outcome and means. Specifically, what are we heading towards? That's the outcome or purpose. And how are we getting there? That's the methods and means.

Consider a simple example. Someone starts a real estate business and looks to employ several agents. In simplest terms, the desired "outcome" is good sales and healthy profits. In the broadest terms, the "means" is to hire good agents and influence them appropriately to achieve the purpose. Thus, the "means" involves organizational structure, policy, procedures, and practices. It also involves specific ways that an owner might choose to influence (motivate) the staff. Some might use bullying or intimidation to coerce their salespeople to drum up more sales in any way possible; even unethical ways. Others might use a system of rewards or accolades to motivate their sales force. Some might model the way forward by joining their staff on the field and working hard alongside them. Others might issue mandates from a plush office and then wait for sales reports at the end of each month or quarter. Several new real estate businesses might launch with similar outcomes in mind, but the leadership "means" (structural and relational ways and methods) can vary enormously.

> We might love the mission of an organization, but we must also be able to tolerate the leadership.

This book is less about the outcomes and more about the means. Ultimately, it's the means that make or break leadership and an organization.

An old adage states that "People join a mission but leave a manager."[18] Unless we're simply grasping for a job to pay the bills, this adage probably rings true. Ideally, we apply to join a company that we love or that shares our values and commitments; perhaps a company that seems to promise a strong future that we find attractive. But we find ourselves working under a boss (manager) who harasses, harangues, or otherwise makes our lives miserable. We might love the purpose (mission) of the organization, but we must also be able to tolerate the leadership. Eventually we might reach a tipping point, whereby the stress (or apathy) caused by management outweighs the sense of accomplishment associated with the mission. And we move on.

The easiest part of leadership is identifying desirable outcomes. Even non-leaders can do this. But *how* we lead towards those outcomes is the defining and difficult dance of leadership. Do we command and control? Are we authoritarian? Should we attempt to be democratic? Do we prefer pace-setting? Have we embraced servant leadership? Do we think more in terms of transactional leadership? What about spiritual leadership? Many possible models have surfaced.

SERVANT LEADERSHIP

Many people (at least since the 1970s) have defined leadership in terms of "servant leadership." The words of Jesus in Matthew 20:27-28 have served as the key text for Christians who embrace this model. *"Whoever wishes to be first among you shall be your slave; just as the Son of Man (Jesus) did not come to be served, but to serve, and to give his life as a ransom for many."*

Many Christians have assumed that secular leadership is fundamentally self-aggrandizing; people wanting to push themselves to the front of the line and seize control. If we start at that point, it follows that the antidote to this kind of self-serving leadership is to serve others. Consequently, we've seen strong advocacy for servant leadership.

On the surface, this seems appropriate, but servant leadership in most circles has been ill-defined. It lacks consistency or clarity, and usually addresses a mindset rather than a methodology (means).

Robert Greenleaf (1904–1990) founded the modern servant-leader movement. After forty years working with AT&T, he concluded that the power-broking authoritarian leadership style that he saw in so many institutions was not working. So, in 1964 he retired and founded the *Greenleaf Center for Servant Leadership*.

In 1970, Greenleaf wrote his first essay titled *"The Leader as Servant."* He would later publish a collection of his essays that has provided a powerful framework for servant leadership.[19] But most people are unfamiliar with his essays and book, and even less familiar with the principles he espoused. Consequently, servant leadership has wallowed in the doldrums for decades, usually reduced to somewhat sappy sentimentality about humility and not much more.

Humility, as we'll see later, has become a major focus of leadership research, and is vital. But on its own, without other core elements to support and frame it, humility proves insufficient. By itself, humility is no predictor or indicator of leadership capacity. Consequently, servant leadership has tended to be strong on service and light on meaningful leadership. It has also often failed to motivate or orchestrate meaningful change.

Nevertheless, in academic circles servant leadership rose to greater heights. Building on Greenleaf's work, various writers defined servant leadership with a range of specific actions, attitudes, and methods. Larry Spears developed ten characteristics of servant leaders based on the writings of Greenleaf. These included: Listening, empathy, healing, awareness, persuasion, conceptualization, foresight, steward-ship, commitment to the growth of others, and building community.[20]

James Sipe and Don Frick reduced these ten elements to seven and concluded that servant leaders "are individuals of character, put people first, are skilled communicators, are compassionate collaborators, use foresight, are systems thinkers, and exercise moral authority."[21]

More recently, Kent Keith added that servant leadership is ethical, practical, and meaningful. He then identified his own seven key practices of servant leaders: Self-awareness, listening, changing the pyramid, developing your colleagues, coaching not controlling, unleashing the energy and intelligence of others, and foresight.[22]

These authors and researchers have tried to flesh out meaningful definitions of servant leadership and as we'll discover, some of their conclusions overlap with the model of transformational leadership.

DEFINING TRANSFORMATIONAL LEADERSHIP

At about the same time that Greenleaf published his book on servant leadership, James MacGregor Burns (1918-2014)—a Pulitzer Prize winner in 1971—wrote the book *Leadership* and proposed another leadership model. He looked at both transactional leadership (give-and-take leadership) and transformational leadership (in which leaders focus on the beliefs, needs, and values of their followers) and decided that they are mutually exclusive. Like oil and water, transactional leadership and transformational leadership simply will not mix. Burns then provided (1978) the first systematic effort to describe and define transformational leadership. Others saw substance and truth in what he wrote and quickly followed his lead.

Seven years later (1985), Bernard M. Bass added to Burns' work. He ultimately identified the four main components of transformational leadership that academics still lean on; sometimes referred to as the four I's.

Idealized Influence—Transformational leaders serve as an ideal role model for their followers. The leader reflects high ethical behavior, instills pride, and lives with authenticity and transparency.

Inspirational Motivation—Transformational leaders have the ability to inspire and motivate followers. They cast vision and help followers develop meaning and purpose for both their own lives and the organization.

Individualized Consideration—Transformational leaders demonstrate genuine concern for the needs and feelings of their followers. This personal attention to each follower is a key element in bringing out their very best.

Intellectual Stimulation—Transformational leaders create space for followers to be innovative and creative, and they constantly challenge followers to higher levels of performance (without compromising a clear moral and ethical standard).

These four phrases appear widely in the academic literature associated with transformational leadership but, for our purposes they seem a little unwieldy and awkward. They speak to profoundly important leadership issues (overlapping with some of the material related to servant leadership), and reflect deep research and consideration. They're just difficult for most of us to readily recall. What if we updated and simplified them just a little?

Idealized Influence = *Authenticity*
Inspirational Motivation = *Inspiration*
Individualized Consideration = *Empathy*
Intellectual Stimulation = *Innovation*

In addition to these four elements, we might also note that change lies at the core of transformational leadership. The inherent nature of transformation is to identify and produce *meaningful* change (not just change for change's sake) and this differentiates transformational leadership from many other leadership models, including servant leadership.

Finally, both Bass and Burns understood (as did Greenleaf) that leadership is more than the successful production or sale of goods and services. Good leadership—leadership for the good of society—must be as concerned with the process (means) as the outcome, and that requires constant attention to the lives of those whom we lead.

If we take these elements and combine them in a fresh way, we might define transformational leadership like this.

TRANSFORMATIONAL LEADERSHIP
Producing change and building lives through
authenticity, inspiration, empathy, and innovation.

This definition provides the outline for the remainder of this book, and we'll examine the implications of each element, particularly from a Christian perspective. Transformational leaders model integrity and honesty. They inspire others collaboratively and frequently. They listen, care, and respond well to everyone within their orbits. And they build cultures of innovation that release creativity, build ownership, and allow for failure.

THE EMERGING LEADERSHIP VACUUM

In 2017, ten thousand baby boomers (people born 1946-1964) were retiring every day.[23] Yes, *every day. Ten thousand.*

This mass retirement movement means that millennials (22-37 year olds in 2018) will constitute nearly half (48 percent) of the workforce by 2020. However, at the time of this writing, 67 percent of the millennials who are currently employed are also actively looking for a *new* job, and most of the remainder expect to be in their current job less than three years. There's not much stability in the workplace.

> *We'll have a shortfall of experienced and well-trained leadership in the next decade, unlike anything we have faced in 50 years.*

Unsurprisingly then, *84 percent of organizations anticipate a shortfall of leaders in the next five years.* That's a dire prognosis, yet only five percent of organizations have implemented strategic and intentional leadership training. That itself is shocking. But wait, there's more.

Currently, only 18 percent of organizations say that their leadership is "very effective" at meeting business goals and only 19 percent of organizations say that they are "very effective" at developing leaders. In short, less than one in five organizations feels "on track" or is doing anything to get "on track" and stay there long-term. Yes, more money is spent on leadership development than any other area of corporate learning, but 71 percent of companies do not feel that their leaders are able to lead the organization into the future.[24]

The numbers are startling, even disturbing. We face a dilemma. We'll have a shortfall of experienced and well-trained leadership in the next decade, unlike anything we have faced in 50 years. And while the millennials are coming through, they do not have clarity on leadership models that are effective and appropriate for their generation or for the world as a whole. That's what makes this conversation about transformational leadership so critically important.

Organizations are wilting. Most have neither training nor succession plans. More to the point, most organizations lack a cohesive model by which to guide and measure leadership development. If that's true, then churches, businesses, and organizations are at the whim of slick conferences and the latest one-off training events. Every best-selling author and book becomes our next new direction. I'd like to suggest that when transformational leadership becomes embedded in our DNA, we will be far more effective as leaders and far less susceptible to the whims of the day.

Transformational leadership is not the latest fad, nor is it an ethereal academic model. It is a well-researched, deeply practical, thoughtful, and proven model for a time such as ours. Interestingly, it also describes the very leadership of Jesus. His revolutionary and prophetic teaching in the first century as well as his life and ministry, align perfectly with the core principles of transformational leadership. This may suggest the timelessness of what we're about to explore more deeply together. Consider the following.

BIBLICAL CONNECTIONS

Transformational leadership describes the life and ministry of Jesus both powerfully and comprehensively. If we use our modified definition of transformational leadership, we find that it aligns with the Gospel (and the gospels) more fully and more thoroughly than other models and definitions. Transformational leadership is deeply consistent with Christian faith and Scripture.

Producing change

The mission and ministry of Jesus was fundamentally, at its core, about change. For example, we might use the biblical word *redemption* to describe his mission. Redemption is not just about claiming us back for God. Nor is just about paying a price for us. It represents something larger. Redemption involves changing our status, changing our lives, changing our destiny, and changing our eternity. Change is written all over it. The apostle Paul chooses language like "new creation" (2 Corinthians 5:17; Galatians 6:15) to describe the change that redemption seeks to produce.

Building lives

The Gospel is not about building a kingdom but building a kingdom *of priests* (Revelation 1:6). God is not so much concerned with sheer numbers, but with personal lives. As we read about the ministry of Jesus, we see story after story of him restoring people physically, socially, emotionally, and spiritually. He brought renewal and hope to people. He gave them purpose and focus. Lives were profoundly changed and remarkably restored. Jesus did not purchase property, erect buildings, or establish an organization. Instead, he invested himself solely and deeply in the well-being of the people around him. He built lives.

Authenticity

What made Jesus so compelling? People certainly were touched by his teaching. They marveled at his ability to heal and to perform miracles. They hoped that he would be able to deliver Israel and free the people and the land from the Roman occupation. But his message also resonated because of his personal authenticity. His life reflected a consistency between his words and his deeds. He lived what he preached, and humility was his hallmark. The Son of God, born in a manger, willing to die on a cross, also lived without needing to exalt himself or seek notoriety.

> *Jesus did not purchase property, erect buildings, or establish an organization. He built lives.*

Nobody could accuse Jesus of living a double-life. He did not lie or deceive. He modeled what he taught. He didn't preach austerity while living in prosperity, He didn't call for morality while hiding a secret side of depravity. Consistency and humility marked his life deeply.

Indeed, the early Church wrote a hymn to extol his humility and the apostle Paul would later embed that hymn into one of his epistles as he urged Christians to "have this mind in you that was in Christ Jesus" — specifically, the attitude of self-emptying and the heart of humility (Philippians 2:5-8).

Inspiration

Jesus cast a fresh vision of the kingdom of God that turned everything upside down. He proclaimed a kingdom where the first would be last and the last would be first; that would be marked by love, not violence; that would be grounded in forgiveness not politics; that would promote grace rather than Law. He used analogies, similes, parables, and metaphors to inspire his followers with this vision. They would no longer band together around ethnicity or tribe. But they would rise to something higher and greater than ever experienced before.

Jesus inspired his followers to look beyond the here and the now, to capture a vision of eternity. He inspired them with words of hope. He called people back to their core identity as sons and daughters of God. He declared to them that God was near, the kingdom of God was at hand, and renewal was coming. And this inspiration powerfully motivated his followers to "produce change and build lives."

Empathy

While Jesus was setting about redeeming humanity, touching lives, being authentic, and casting a vision for the kingdom of God, he also modeled profound empathy. He walked among the people rather than sitting in an office and gathering reports about the people. He listened to them. He cried with them. He talked with them. He blessed them. And all of this because, as we read in several places, he was "filled with compassion" for them (Matthew 9:36; 14:14; 15:32; 20:34). His ministry was not only *for* people but *with* people and *to* people. Empathy, in all of its richest nuances, marked the ministry of Jesus.

We read a short but powerful story in Mark 1:40-42 about Jesus meeting a leper. Jesus had been traveling among the villages of Galilee, speaking in the synagogues, when a man with leprosy came to him, falling on his knees and begging Jesus, "If you are willing, you can make me clean." This leper had no business approaching a renowned rabbi. A simple touch would render Jesus unclean. More than that, if Jesus contracted leprosy it would derail his entire ministry. If he came down with this dreaded disease he would be required to live in isolation from the community. This was a moment fraught with danger. But the Scripture says that Jesus, far from being filled with apprehension or

> *Jesus walked among the people rather than sitting in an office and gathering reports about the people.*

fear was "filled with compassion" and said to the man "I am willing. Be clean!" And immediately the leprosy left the man and he was cleansed.

This kind of empathy became the hallmark of Jesus' ministry. He did not throw out miracles randomly like candy tossed to children at Halloween. He listened. He empathized. He entered the world and the pain of the people. He looked them in the eye, and responded to them with grace. He dignified them. Just as importantly, this empathy ("individualized consideration") served a greater goal—fully engaged followers fulfilling their calling to get the mission accomplished. Empathy does not serve as an end in itself, but as an authentic, relational means to empower others to fulfill the mission.

Innovation

Jesus, arguably, brought the greatest innovation and released the greatest innovation, in human history. This is true at multiple levels.

The apostle John understood Jesus to be the very creator and innovator of all that is. He wrote of Jesus: "All things came into being through him, and apart from him nothing came into being that has come into being" (John 1:3, NASB).

The apostle Paul made similar claims in his epistle to the Colossians: "By him all things are created, both in the heavens and on earth, visible and invisible, whether thrones or dominions or rulers or authorities — all things have been created through him and for him" (Colossians 1:16).

The early Church viewed Christ as the Creator, the one who creates *ex nihilo*, who is the great Innovator. But at a secondary level, Jesus also transformed common structures into novel new structures. He took the ancient Israelite *qahal* (assembly) and the ancient Greek *ekklesia* (assembly) and gave them dramatically new meaning as he formed the Church. He took the ancient Jewish Passover meal and transformed its significance and meaning into something which pointed to himself and the cross. He proclaimed a new covenant to supersede the old one, but as a remarkable fulfillment of all that went before, not a mere dismissal.

Innovation is core to the person, work, and ministry of Jesus. Subsequently, his people have spent centuries inventing and implementing innovative structures (consistent with the kingdom of God) to catapult human experience forward. Jesus did the unthinkable, proclaiming a kingdom that would not require conversion to Judaism (or any ethnic group or religious system in existence).

The Gospel has resulted in men and women who have shaped human history in extraordinary ways; educational systems, hospitals, suffragette movements, civil rights movements, scientific developments, legal systems, and economic models, to name just a few. All of this innovation has been spawned by faith and by very specific kingdom values.

As we overlay transformational leadership and the ministry of Jesus, we see extraordinary parallels. This model for leadership provides tremendous insights into the core traits of Christ and his kingdom.

CHAPTER SUMMARY

We can succinctly reduce leadership to outcomes and means. What are we trying to achieve and how are we getting there? But it involves a greater complexity. Consequently, people have been studying leadership seriously for the past fifty years. Many Christians have settled on servant leadership as the best model to embrace, but transformational leadership better describes the life and ministry of Jesus, and better prepares us for the leadership challenges and opportunities that faces us in the days ahead.

NOTES

Key thoughts you had while reading this chapter. **Questions** that came up. **Ideas** for personal next steps. **Insights** to discuss with a friend.

_____

_____

_____

_____

_____

_____

Chapter 2

Producing Change

"One does not discover new lands without consenting to lose sight of the shore for a very long time." – Andre Gide

Many people have observed that the only constant in life is change. Despite appearances, nothing really sits still. Living organisms are growing, dying, and changing constantly. But the same might be said of organizations. Nothing is truly static.

We might accurately say that the *rate of change* varies enormously, but change is still the constant. Kevin Cashman writes:

> We operate under the illusion that life remains constant, but in reality everything is always changing. From breath to breath, we exchange so many atoms we change the makeup of our physiology in a moment. In the course of one year, 98 percent of all our atoms are exchanged for new ones; we are literally new people each year.[25]

If human beings are always changing—our bodies, knowledge, values, relationships, and even our faith—then the organizations made up of human beings and even culture itself is inevitably surging back and forth all the time, like a massive tide.

Change is all around us, and the rate of change is accelerating far beyond anything experienced in former generations. The move from the industrial age to the information/technology age, and now to the innovation age has been blindingly fast and our church structures, educational models, business practices, and medical ethics (indeed, nearly every sphere of life) suddenly seem inadequate.

In his renowned book *Leading Change*, John Kotter argues that managing change and leading change are two very different matters. Management, in his view, is about keep established systems running smoothly (budgets, organizing, staffing, controlling, and problem solving). But leadership creates organizations in the first place. It adapts to changing pressures and circumstances. It defines what the future should look like. Kotter writes:

> *Managing change is important; leading change matters even more.*

> Managing change is important. Without competent management, the transformation process can get out of control. But for most organizations, the much bigger challenge is leading change.[26]

Our turbulent times require men and women who not only manage change but lead change—people who *produce change*. It doesn't help to watch from a distance and tut-tut about how fast everything is morphing or complain about the peril we might be facing. Arm-chair critics and disengaged experts abound. The real need of our day is leaders—transformational leaders—who can identify and produce the changes needed to keep the ship steady in the storm. We need leaders who can point the way through. We need leaders who are adaptive.

As a kid, I enjoyed playing chess. We had chess tournaments when I was in 5th and 6th grade, and those of us who wanted to play would line up across from each other during recess and lunch and compete. Those were fun times, but the clock was ticking and the bell was also threatening to ring and ruin our game. I quickly learned that offense was the best form of defense. When people are on the back foot, they rarely collect themselves to mount an attack. If I saw my opponent coming after me, I'd try to strike first. Take the initiative. Throw them off-balance. Distract them and force a change. This strategy won me a lot of games.

Transformational leaders understand this. They know that their first charge—their first responsibility as leaders—involves taking the initiative and leading change.

The status quo, keeping things as they have always been, is eventually a failing formula built on a false assumption that people and culture are neither touched nor deeply influenced by the radical and cataclysmic pace of change around us. While traditions absolutely play a role in keeping families, churches, and communities grounded and connected, leading towards the past is the surest way to ensure there is no future. Indeed, our leadership effectiveness is in direct proportion to our ability to adapt to change and initiate change before outdated models, policies, and practices render us obsolete and ineffective.

However, as Robert Kegan and Lisa Laskow Lahey have written, human beings (that would be all of us) have a fundamental immunity to change.[27] Anyone who has tried to lead others through change knows that this is no simple task. It's the first task of the transformational leader, and simultaneously an enormously difficult task.

Various pundits have studied why leading change seems so difficult. They cite lack of urgency, inadequate support, lack of vision, and institutional resistance to change. Correspondingly, they write about creating urgency, providing incentives, and building a compelling vision. If we can just get these three elements in play, we'll be able to instigate and lead change, they say. But much deeper issues are at play.

> Not long ago a medical study showed that if heart doctors tell their seriously at-risk patients they will literally die if they do not make changes to their personal lives — diet, exercise, smoking — still only one in seven is actually able to make the changes. One in seven! And we can safely assume that the other six wanted to live, see more sunsets, watch their grandchildren grow up. They didn't lack a sense of urgency. The incentives for change could not be greater. The doctors made sure they knew just what they needed to do. Still, they couldn't do it.[28]

Similarly, 50-75 percent of smoking cessation and weight-loss programs don't succeed. It would be incorrect to say that people just changed their minds because they actually felt good about their wheezing lungs or obesity.

As transformational leaders, before we oversimplify (or understate) the call to change or the process of change, we need to understand the fundamental immunity to change — the inertia — all around us and within us. Yes, on the one hand change is a constant in our lives, but on the other hand immunity to change is just as real.

Effective change-leadership does not seek to smash a thimble with a sledge-hammer, but grasps the nuances of "producing change." It recognizes the power of culture (in a family, church, or corporation) and it embraces the truth that change is most often the product of a thousand small steps not a single leap into a new future.

IMMUNITY TO CHANGE

Anyone who has served in leadership has run up against naysayers. We've all met those people who just don't like change and who resist it actively. Sometimes those folk will speak up to our face, other times we hear secondhand about their subversive conversations with other people. One way or another they are "the vocal opposition."

But there's a second group, the passive-aggressive team members (or congregational members) who say little or nothing but they've made up their mind and simply won't step up and support the new initiative. They go about their lives (and jobs) and want nothing to do with the changes in the wind. They smile politely, and nod gently as we talk with them, then seem like immovable objects.

Finally, there's a third group; perhaps the most surprising group of all. These folk assure us of their support. They smile and applaud the presentation of new ideas. They affirm our leadership, and for a while they sit in meetings and speak positively, but then (almost inexplicably) they just seem to run out of gas.

In the end, we can clump most people into one of these three main categories, and we hope that the vocal opposition is small, the passive aggressors are relatively few, and the "supporters" outnumber the other two groups combined. All the while, however, we may have failed to understand the dynamics of change and become discouraged when the initiative limps along or grinds to a standstill.

Consider the human body for a moment. We have an immune system that is finely tuned to ward off nasty cells. When bacteria, viruses, or cancers attack our bodies, we have white blood cells that immediately go to war. This is vitally important for human health and our well-being. If every new and strange cell could take up residence and do what it wants within us, we'd die quickly. We don't have to consciously send our white cells to work. It just happens. They just kick into gear and do their job. The immune system protects us, usually without us even knowing it's at work.

The analogy holds surprisingly true of corporate bodies (families, churches, businesses, and schools) too.

We're inclined to think that opponents to our ideas are simply grouchy personalities or selfish individuals who are either out of touch or power-hungry. In fact, what we have at play is a social version of the biological reality we all experience every day. Kegan and Lahey put it this way:

> In some instances an immune system [surprisingly] can threaten our continued good health. When it rejects new material, internal or external to the body [for example, an organ transplant or skin graft] that the body needs to heal itself or to thrive, the immune system can put us in danger. In these instances, the immune system is no less

focused on protecting us. It is just making a mistake. It does not understand that it must alter its code. It does not understand that, ironically, in working to protect us, it is actually putting us at serious risk.... Change does not fail to occur because of insincerity. The heart patient is not insincere about his wish to keep living, even as he reaches for another cigarette. Change fails to occur because we mean *both* things. It fails to occur because we are a living contradiction.[29]

In short, most of us live with both a foot on the gas and a foot on the brake at the same time. We want a strong future, but we don't want to lose what we've got. And that's normal. Transformational leaders know that producing change is not without these complex social and personal contradictions.

The old adage that "people just don't like change" is a half-truth at best. If we tell a single and lonely young man that he'll have a girlfriend tomorrow, or a young married woman wanting a child that next month she will be pregnant, these are not likely to cause undue stress or be resisted. Many changes we welcome. The issue is not change alone but, more specifically, *change that leaves us feeling defenseless in the face of apparent dangers.*

> *The old adage that people just don't like change, is only a half-truth at best.*

When we encounter resistance to change, the solution is not necessarily to quickly remove or run over the people who openly resist change. It involves much deeper adaptive changes, first within ourselves as leaders and then within the social structures we lead.

In short, all of us carry a complex web of systems within us—a *knowing system* (how we organize reality), *a feeling system* (how we manage anxiety), and *a change-prevention system* (how we intuitively protect ourselves against loss).[30] This means that effective change-leadership is not merely a matter of driving a truck through a narrow doorway, but addressing these personal and corporate systems. People always resist change when the following happens:

1. They have insufficient knowledge to be able to make sense of the "new reality";
2. They have insufficient confidence to overcome the anxiety associated with their place in the new reality;
3. They intuitively sense — even if they can't articulate it with words — that this change will mean significant loss either corporately or personally.

There's much more to be said about this, but suffice it to say that producing change, as we'll see, requires authenticity, inspiration, empathy, innovation, and patience.[31]

Of course, we see increasing numbers of small church congregations grappling with changing demographics (aging population, diverse communities, and shifts in social values). Many of these congregations persist for years — in some cases decades — without much vitality, but they will close their doors permanently in the next few years. Hopefully, as they close out their life-cycle they will do so both "on purpose" and "with purpose." Remaining safely locked in time is simply not an option.

Transformational leaders function with the conviction that nothing is yet what it could be, or will need to be. It's not simply that "our greatest days are still ahead of us." That may or may not be true. But this we can say with true confidence: Maintaining the status quo, holding everything in check, surely means that our *toughest* days lie ahead. Corporate By-laws and constitutions do not guarantee our future. They just help us wind up a business in an orderly way.

In the Age of Innovation, which describes our own time, transformational leaders know that their primary leadership calling involves producing change despite the deeply ingrained immunity to change which we both encounter and sometimes display.

TECHNICAL CHANGE & ADAPTIVE CHANGE

One of the keys to producing change involves recognizing the important distinction between technical change and adaptive change. Transformational leaders focus significantly on the latter, while many of us get caught trying to manage (almost exclusively) the former.

For example, if a company or business implements new sales software, immense amounts of energy get expended simply ensuring that everyone can use the new software. This is "technical change." It's the ability to develop new technical skills to meet a pressing need or demand. In an educational environment, the technical skill might relate to monitoring compliance issues and reporting on them. Do teachers know how to collate their assessment reports? Does everyone understand basic policies, procedures, and practices? Are the systems all working smoothly? All of this pertains to technical change.

Technical change involves teaching people pre-existent skills; removing a gall bladder, repairing a plane engine, managing mutual funds, selling insurance products, etc. These are all vital skills. I'd certainly want a doctor who knows the difference between my gall bladder and my kidneys. But it's the stuff of management, not transformational leadership. It doesn't create anything new. It simply ensures that everyone on the factory floor is doing their job, and that no gaps develop in the systems that exist.

Adaptive change, on the other hand, as you might imagine is considerably different. Adaptive change is not about building skillsets to consistently serve existing systems. Rather, like the men of Issachar of old, "men who understood the times and knew what Israel should do" (1 Chronicles 12:32), adaptive change involves

> *Adaptive change looks beyond the present and builds a better future.*

looking beyond what is here and now and building for a better future—not just more of the same done with greater efficiency, but new things. The innovation age begs for this kind of leadership; transformational leadership.

Adaptive change no doubt requires a higher level of mental complexity. Our capacity to analyze current practices, read a need, identify a trend, anticipate emerging opportunities, and design solutions is definitely not low-level complexity. And the capacity to motivate people in these new directions is no small matter either. But this is what we mean by "producing change" as transformational leaders.

If you're currently in leadership, how much of your time and attention gets consumed addressing technical changes? And how much energy have you devoted to establishing a culture of adaptive change in your team? This is not just the prerogative of entrepreneurs and their high-risk partners. This is the leadership that any of us can embrace. This is the leadership that changes communities.

I'm not suggesting that technical change is unimportant. Not at all. Failure to manage technical change within an organization (or a family) would be the most elementary failure of all. As we are raising our kids, we *must* teach them basic skills—how to cook, basic cleaning and maintenance skills, financial literacy, and so on. But managing adaptive change within our kids means that we help them explore college programs and potential careers perhaps well beyond our own experience. It means teaching them to manage technology and think theologically and ethically in a world that is radically different from 30 years ago. These are not technical skills but adaptive skills.

What we do ideally with our families is also what we must consider ideally within our churches and organizations. Technical change is important when we're onboarding new people into our setting. But adaptive change lays the foundation for future vision and thriving groups of people.

SWOT ➡ SWT

The distinction between technical and adaptive change might also be captured by the difference between SWOT analysis and SWT analysis.

Verne Harnish is the founder of Gazelles, a global executive education, coaching, and technology firm. He proposes that we supplement (not replace) the traditional SWOT analysis with a SWT analysis.

For many years, leaders have done SWOT analyses of their organizations: Strengths, Weaknesses, Opportunities, and Threats. This has been standard fare for business coaches and consultants, and at a lower level of leadership it serves a useful purpose. However, as Harnish notes, "the SWOT process drives leaders to look inward at both their company and industry challenges, creating what we call 'inside/industry myopia.' The traditional SWOT analysis, while helping executives see the forest and the trees, tends to lead them to forget that there's a world outside the forest."[32]

By contrast, the SWT analysis lifts leaders out of the weeds as they consider: Strengths, Weaknesses, and *Trends*. Transformational leaders rise above the introspective analysis and give particular attention to significant changes happening culturally as well as within the "industry." Then they lead to not only address the weakness and threats they face, but to determine whether the trends might even render those things obsolete in the near future. Let me give two examples.

Churches are notoriously as slow to make adaptive change as any other organization—perhaps moreso, when their leadership has been seminary-trained. Many seminaries are habitually 15-20 years behind the cultural and educational curve.[33] Consequently, we see many congregations failing to use technology to reach and serve people, failing to address the particular human needs arising in the technological and innovative age, and failing to make their message (Scripture and Gospel) relevant to the emerging generations. Instead, some churches seem to consider it a badge of honor to resist (or deny) cultural trends.

Families can be just as myopic. It's easy for parents to identify the strengths, opportunities, weaknesses, and threats to their kids. Increasing numbers of Christian families (and others) are choosing to home-school their kids because of what they perceive as threats. In a sense, some of the home-schooling movement (not all, by any means) aims to produce technical change (teaching how to read, write, research, and do math) without always acknowledging the need for adaptive change (social media management, ethical adaptations and applications, and leadership in a world of uncertainty).

Transformational leaders in every sphere—business leaders, pastors, and parents—give increasing attention to the

> *Fads pass but trends define.*

trends and the adaptive changes needed to create a better future for those whom they lead. But they also know to distinguish between trends and fads. Fads are passing; trends are defining. YoYo's, fidget-spinners, Chia-heads, and bell-bottom jeans are all fads. They came, made a brief splash, and flamed out quickly. If you were fast enough to invest early *and sell early* in these fads you might have made some quick money. But trends are altogether different.

We still talk about digital immigrants (anyone over 30 years old) and digital natives (anyone under 20). The former have had to make technical changes; learn how to use technology. The latter engage with digital media intuitively; many of them with brains that are literally re-wired by the hours they've spent immersed in the digital world since they were the smallest of children.[34] As someone once quipped, "If you want to understand life ask an older person. If you want to understand how the world works, ask a younger person!"

The digital age is no fad. It's no longer even a trend. It is simply the new reality, deeply entrenched and ubiquitous in our lives. Yet, so many organizations still spend money on roadside billboards (which nobody can read quickly enough or really make note of) rather than targeted social media campaigns using Facebook, Twitter, Snapchat, and other platforms. What trends have you identified that need to inform your changes?

As human beings, we experience change every day. As transformational leaders, we want to delineate between technical and adaptive change, and between fads and trends. But the human dynamics involved in change are not new. Change is not particular or peculiar to our age. Jesus himself came with a message of change. He upset both familial and political structures, as he sought to produce *good* change.

THE CHRISTIAN GOSPEL AND CHANGE

Jesus did not come with the message: "The kingdom of God is at hand...and nothing's going to change." Indeed, he began his ministry with the single statement, "Repent, for the kingdom of the heavens is at hand" (Matthew 4:17). The word "repent" drips with the notion of change. We have often associated it purely with contrition over sin. Repentance, we've concluded, is sorrow for sin. It should reflect grief for the sinful things we have thought, said, or done. But biblically, repentance has a much broader meaning. The Greek term (*metanoia*) has little to do with sadness. It literally means "to change the mind." It means to think differently, to change our perspective, to change direction (because we have changed our mind). It's not an "I'm sorry" but an "I'm changing the way I live." And this is how Jesus opened up his ministry; calling people to change their minds and change their lives because God's expansive kingdom, which transcends all of the heavens is about to break into human history like never before.

Not only did Jesus commence his ministry with this call to change, but he continued to challenge his listeners throughout his ministry. Time and again, he insisted that people not return to old ways but embrace new ways.

> *Not only did Jesus commence his ministry with a call to change, but he continued this challenge and call throughout his ministry.*

In John 8:1-11 we read about a woman caught in adultery who is then dragged before Jesus. It's all an elaborate trap by the religious leaders of the day; an attempt to compromise Jesus and bring him down. But at the end of the story, when Jesus has vanquished the accusers, he turns to the woman and says, "Neither do I condemn you. Go now and leave your life of sin." He delivers her, but calls her to change.

Earlier, in John 5:39-40, Jesus had tussled with the religious elite and challenged their closed-mindedness: "You study the Scriptures diligently because you think that in them you have eternal life. These are the very Scriptures that testify about me, yet you refuse to come to me to have life." The religious elite had settled into a comfortable religious system that served their purposes well enough. They did not want upheaval. The message of Jesus threatened their status quo, so they naturally resisted him. That's why Nicodemus, one of the wealthy elite ("a man of the Pharisees, and a ruler of the Jews") but curious about Christ, came to Jesus under cover of darkness (John 3:1-2). The entire establishment was resistant to change. They knew that the message of Jesus would overturn everything.

Change. Change. Change.

The New Testament epistles are also replete with a call to change. The apostle Paul urged his readers to "consider yourselves now dead to sin but alive to God through Christ Jesus" (Romans 6:11). Could there be any greater change than to die to ourselves?

Paul would also write about putting off certain practices (anger, wrath, malice, slander, etc.) and putting on replacement behaviors (compassion, kindness, humility, gentleness, etc.).[35] Indeed, James, Peter, John, and other New Testament writers constantly called their readers to lay aside destructive practices and attitudes, and embrace more Christ-like, God-honoring, and kingdom-consistent ways. Nobody in the early Church could conceive that a person might become a Christian and not change.

In more theological terms we call this *sanctification* — the process of being changed "from glory to glory" (2 Corinthians 3:18). This is the most meaningful change imaginable. Lives change. Marriages and families change. Communities change. And ultimately cultures change.

Daily change lies at the heart of God's work within us and plan for us. As we partner with him, we'll embrace change as the norm for both life and leadership.

CHAPTER SUMMARY

The primary task of the transformational leader is to produce meaningful change. This requires both finesse and wisdom, but also an understanding of the fundamental differences between managing technical change and driving adaptive change. Furthermore, transformational leadership moves beyond identifying strengths, weaknesses, opportunities, and threats. It grapples with important trends. Fads pass; trends define. But we all carry an immunity to change. It's not resistance for its own sake. Transformational leaders understand this immunity not as obstructionism but as a survival mechanism or loss-management system inherent within people, and they produce change with sensitivity to these dynamics.

SOME POSSIBLE EXERCISES

Technical & Adaptive Change

Make a list of changes you currently face or would like to implement in your setting (business, school, church, or home). Which of these changes are technical changes? Which are adaptive changes? What does this list tell you?

SWOT ➡ SWT

What are five *important* trends that are affecting your business, church, or home right now? What are your current strengths and weaknesses? How might you best produce change?

Immunity to Change

If you're seeking to produce change at the moment (in your employees, staff, or family) what are some of the potential losses that might activate "immunity to change" in other people? Make a list. Identify one or two next steps to address this.

NOTES

Key thoughts you had while reading this chapter. **Questions** that came up. **Ideas** for personal next steps. **Insights** to discuss with a friend.

_____

_____

_____

_____

_____

_____

Chapter 3

Building Lives

"Outstanding leaders go out of their way to boost the self-esteem of their personnel. If people believe in themselves, it's amazing what they can accomplish." – Sam Walton

Transformational leadership focuses first and foremost on people, not budgets and buildings. It refers not to how many people we lead, but to the quality of the lives of those we lead. There's a huge difference.

Many leaders assume that the measure of their success is related to the *number* of people they lead—"I have four people in my department." "I lead a team of twelve." "I have thirty salespeople working for me." Some parents might even feel more accomplished if they have raised more children than their peers.

Transformational leaders understand that the core question is not "How many people do I lead?" but the deeper question "How many people flourish under my leadership?" The difference between these two questions is enormous. Transformational leadership reflects a commitment to building the lives of both our teams and our customers or clients. Financial profits matter, but greenbacks and coins matter far less than lives.

"Building lives" means that we create structures and environments, policies and practices, organizational priorities and cultures that enhance the well-being of *everyone* involved. We build lives when we provide adequate compensation and benefits for people, so they can live without fear of injury or illness. We build lives when we know people by name, listen to them, and care about them. We build lives when we help those around us flourish, whether that be a spouse, a child, a friend, a colleague, or a worker. People flourish when others recognize and appreciate them. We flourish when people value us. We flourish when we are treated with respect and honor. We flourish when we are treated with dignity and equality. These are just some of the ways that transformational leaders "build lives."

> A core question: "How many people flourish under my leadership?"

The flourishing life does not require exorbitant financial safety nets or constant job promotions or the plushest office. These may be nice, but flourishing lives reflect a well-being of the soul; lives with manageable stress or fear; lives with hope and purpose; lives with joy and meaningful human connection. Too many families, churches, and organizations understand this intuitively, but fail to pursue or practice it.

Transformational leaders, those who live into this calling and responsibility, place "building lives" — building *flourishing* lives — front and center to everything. They produce change and build lives. It's what they do.

As a church planter, this truth was easy to affirm but surprisingly difficult to apply. I felt the pressure to make the church financially stable. I faced the constant challenge of whether to pursue people who could serve and give generously, or get involved in the messiness of some of our neediest souls. Financial stresses certainly tempted me (and others) to see and assess people as "giving units." Transformational leadership, however, prioritizes people ahead of products, and focuses first on lives rather than budget line items.

This also applies in our marriages and families. Leadership belongs there as much as anywhere. Would it change our attitudes and choices if we committed to "building lives" in our marriage and family? If we set out intentionally to build the life of our spouse, might it re-shape some of our decisions? With our kids, we often want to build a better financial and material future for them than we might have had. But this sometimes degenerates into a focused pursuit of wealth and resources. Ironically, it does little or nothing to actually build the lives of our kids, who need our attention, affection, connection, and presence more than they need a 529 College Savings Plan.

Businesses don't fare much better. So many business leaders constantly review the financial bottom line which does not paint any kind of picture of the hurts, joys, aspirations, or hopes of the workers. "We've got a job to do, and we're here to do it," some people declare with great clarity. But when the job becomes disconnected from the lives and feelings of the followers we lose something central to transformational leadership.

In his bestseller *Leaders Eat Last*, renowned leadership guru Simon Sinek writes:

Sadly, it is common for leaders of companies to see the people as the means to drive the numbers. The leaders of great organizations do not see people as a commodity to be managed to help grow the money. They see the money as the commodity to be managed to help grow their people.[36]

When generating revenue supplants building the people, leadership loses its way. The shift happens gradually and sometimes imperceptibly. It may not become evident until a crisis arrives. But when faithful, loyal, and diligent people become expendable because of financial exigency, the leadership culture needs a fresh look.

The Church is not immune to these same temptations. Historically, the Church has described pastoral leadership as "the cure of souls." This image perfectly captures the heart of ministry. But today we see a dramatic shift in many congregations. It has become more commonplace to speak about "running the church" than "the cure of souls."[37] The language matters. It indicates a significant philosophical change; a profound alteration of priorities. Spiritual nurture has given way to program development, at substantial cost to the spiritual depth of the church. Celebrity pastors may carry the title of pastor but function more like CEOs or stage stars. There's little surprise that when "building lives" gets tossed to the side, that performance worship and spectator congregations sweep into existence. Yet, the cure of souls, in some respects is not just an ancient Church tradition but the fundamental call of all transformational leadership.

In July 2014 William Deresiewicz published an article in *New Republic* titled "Don't Send Your Kid to The Ivy League." He called out elitist educational institutions, criticizing their admissions practices and educational priorities, and concluded that college education should be a *"soul-enriching experience."* The article certainly got the attention of readers. It generated more than two million online hits and received more comments (and controversy) than any article in the *New Republic*'s one-hundred-year history.

It's the reference to *"soul-enriching experience"* that surprised me. We typically associate the education industry with intellectual stimulation and competency development. But *soul-enrichment*? Even the acknowledgment of a soul would be progress for some leaders. Yet, the sooner we start to see the humanity of those around us, the

> The sooner we start to see the humanity of those around us, the better.

better. This *soul-enrichment* lies at the heart of building lives; helping people flourish and thrive at every level of their being.

Google has tackled this (in part) by reframing its Human Resources Department into the People Operations Team. The shift of language is significant. It humanizes everyone. By changing the name from the usual black-and-white corporate-speak, Google emphasizes that it employs people, not machines.

Of course, it's entirely understandable why many leaders end up de-humanizing their workforce. It makes the followers far less attached and far more expendable. The less connected we are with people (emotionally, socially, and spiritually), the easier it is to treat them poorly (with poor pay, conditions, or exploitation) or fire them. The infamous sweat-shops of Asia provide a classic example of de-humanizing others who are distant from us. The less we see them, talk with them, or interact with them, the easier we find it to exploit them.

In war, each side of the conflict constantly de-humanizes the other, so that fighters won't baulk at their duty. So, we call each other "enemy combatants" or just "the enemy." When we replace given names (first names and family names) with cold labels, we steadily distance ourselves from others. When we treat people as abstractions rather than as sons, daughters, husbands, wives, or parents, we reduce the emotional connection we might have with them.

Transformational leaders refuse to settle for such isolation. They reject the assumption that "building lives" is the exclusive domain of spiritual leaders or pastors. *All* leaders carry responsibility for the flourishing of those whom they lead.

In early 2018, my colleague Dr. Daniel Gluck published a powerful blog post titled "The End of Poverty." He suggested that we will not eradicate poverty (which afflicts roughly one billion people in the world) by simply bolstering financial aid. Indeed, the billions of dollars sent annually to the most impoverished places on the planet, seem to have done relatively little to alleviate the plight of the poor. Rather, "financial distress is only one aspect of poverty. Poverty is emotional, spiritual, physical, social, and political." To quote Bryant Myers (*Walking with the Poor*) "poverty, in its essence, is when someone does not know who they are, or for what purpose they were created."[38]

Leaders often spend huge amounts of time, energy, and money trying to fix systems, without realizing that the real solution also involves building purpose, meaning, love, and connection for the people within the system.

In an extraordinary June 2015 TED Talk, Johann Hari spoke on the topic *"Everything you think you know about addiction is wrong."* Hari's 14-minute talk was watched by over 8.7 million people in the following 30 months. He presented research and compelling evidence to show that addictions (drugs, alcohol, sex, and medications) are much less biologically-driven than socially-driven. Hari concludes that the solution to drug addiction is not to criminalize drug use and further alienate and isolate the user by tossing them in prison, but to restore their social connections whereby they feel significance, love, and value. Research conclusively demonstrates that when people feel disconnected or isolated from other people, they have high susceptibility to addictions. They are most vulnerable when they are alone.[39]

Transformational leaders have an extraordinary opportunity (and perhaps obligation) to create environments where people connect and flourish. Hostile workplaces—even apathetic and disconnected workplaces—not only minimize productivity but damage people. Part of the joy of transformational leadership involves creating a meaningful community environment (work, church, or family) that diminishes the attraction of addictive alternatives.

GIVERS, TAKERS, & MATCHERS

In his New York Times bestseller *Give and Take*, Adam Grant shares some surprising research. He broadly divides people into one of three categories—givers, takers, or matchers. Takers like to take more from people than they give. They are competitive and self-protective, cautious and self-promoting, manipulative and self-serving. Givers tilt the reciprocity the other way, preferring to give more to others than they get. Matchers tend to seek an equal balance between giving and taking, exchanging favors; "You scratch my back and I'll scratch yours." Matchers practice transactional leadership.

Which of these three groups fares most poorly in the workplace?

Research affirms exactly what you might expect. The givers tend to sink to the bottom of the success ladder. People take advantage of them. They give up their shirts and lose their place in line. Self-sacrificial givers don't fare well.

Which of the three groups fares best in the workplace?

Well, here's the surprise. Neither of the remaining two groups—neither the takers nor the matchers—take top place. That's right. Neither of them. At the top of the success ladder, are the givers. Yes, they occupy both the top *and* the bottom rungs.[40]

Research shows that takers do not typically make for good transformational leaders. Their self-serving orientation to life blinds them to the needs of others, and minimizes any genuine commitment to building up other people. The research also indicates that they ultimately have little sustainable leadership impact.

Similarly, matchers fall in the middle of the pack. Transactional leadership—simply trading favors—proves too objective and detached from the real human element. While matchers appear less self-serving than takers, the difference is ultimately marginal.

The givers win the day.

What does this suggest? Well, it highlights that a focus on building others has a surprising reciprocity. When we build others — especially with boundaries to protect our own mental and emotional health — we flourish, as do others. This lies at the heart of transformational leadership.

Of course, the term *boundaries* is the key. Givers who fail to identify and sustain healthy personal boundaries generally suffer. They get overwhelmed and burned out. On the other hand, givers with a sacrificial inclination, who genuinely desire the well-being and welfare of others, but who also maintain good personal boundaries for self-preservation commonly rise to the top.

PRODUCING MORE LEADERS

Ralph Nader, the renowned American political activist, author, lecturer, and attorney, once noted that "the function of leadership is to produce more leaders, not more followers."[41] This defies the experience common of many of us. We've all met or watched leaders trying to build their own kingdoms, expand their personal influence, and produce more *followers*. We may have (somewhat innocently) done that ourselves, but Nader proposes that a chief end of good leadership is to produce other good *leaders*. He's correct, of course, but his statement needs a small adjustment.

The function of good leadership is not simply to find and release other people who are willing to take charge and give the orders. The function of good leadership is constantly to raise up transformational leaders who genuinely love those whom they lead; leaders who will not only produce change but who will do so while also building the lives of those whom they lead. This requires several core qualities in the transformational leader.

1. Security

Some people pursue leadership *to find* security; others step up to leadership *because of* their security. There's a world of difference between the two. Insecure leadership is marked by territorialism, suspicion, competition, and selfish ambition. Secure leadership — core to true transformational leadership — models generosity, trust, collaboration, and humility.

Insecure leadership generally develops from poor examples, bad experiences, or stunted personal development. That's not to say that these people can't achieve remarkable success. Narcissism — an almost pathological self-absorption which requires constant affirmation and is "always right" — holds back some leaders; but not all.

Is it possible to shake off insecurity and develop security? Absolutely. Insecurity is more than a personality trait. It's a deeply ingrained habit; a way of thinking and a way of life to unlearn. Ultimately, security is also a profoundly spiritual issue, usually tied directly to identity. Insecure leaders are generally in an endless quest to assert themselves so that they feel powerful. They unconsciously function on the premise that power and authority will fill the identity gap. Those who have complete confidence in their identity, are far better positioned to be patient, content, settled, and able to see the landscape of the lives they lead.

One of the most profound Gospel stories comes at the very start of Jesus' ministry. Before he performs his first miracle, he goes to the Jordan River to be baptized by his cousin, John the Baptizer (Matthew 3:13-17). As Matthew tells the story, when Jesus comes up out of the water, "The heavens were opened, and John saw the Spirit of God descending like a dove and resting upon Jesus, and a voice out of the heavens said, 'This is my beloved son, in whom I am well-pleased.'"

It's a powerful and crucial starting point for Jesus. As he now sets his face toward a three-year ministry and then the Cross, it's vital that he begin with a deep certainty about his identity. All sorts of trials and false-voices will seek to distract him in the three years to follow, but for Jesus to have utter security in his identity is imperative. "This is my beloved son," said God. That's far more than a divine "Good job!" Jesus hears direct affirmation of his identity—crucial to his ministry *from* security instead of ministry *for* security. He has no need to prove himself to anyone. Nor does he need affirmation from anyone else. His Father's approval and love will sustain him entirely.

Transformational leadership depends on clarity of our identity, which produces depth to our security. But raising up other leaders, and not feeling threatened by them, also requires a good dose of trust.

2. *Trust*

Building people means first and foremost building trust between people. In his best-selling book *The Five Dysfunctions of a Team*, Patrick Lencioni makes a powerful case for trust being the bedrock of all strong and healthy teams.[42] He presents five dysfunctions which build on each other and have deep inter-connections.

The bedrock of dysfunction in any gathering of people (a marriage, family, church, or company) is *"absence of trust"* which leads to *"fear of conflict."* Eventually, the inability to communicate openly for fear of conflict, leads to a *"lack of commitment"* which then spawns *"avoidance of accountability."* In any place where trust is missing, we fear conflict, we lack commitment, and we avoid accountability. We also experience *"inattention to results."* In short, if we cannot trust each other, the inevitable outcome will be either breakdown of the team (people leaving) or collapse of our productivity (people just skating under the radar).[43]

> *Trust does not form when leaders constantly put "spin" on their statements.*

Trust, then, forms the heartbeat of health, and transformational leaders understand how core it is to not only building an organization, but to building the lives of those on the team.

Trust takes a long time to build, and a moment to shatter. It's also far easier to build trust than to re-build it. But trust depends on truth. We cannot build trust with others by lying *to* them or *about* them. Trust does not form when leaders constantly put "spin" on their statements. That's why transparency, vulnerability, and honesty are core to any culture of trust. When we sacrifice these three qualities, we quickly start to decline. As many people have found, it's far easier to build trust than to re-build it.

How do we build trust, as transformational leaders committed to building lives? With patience, with consistency, with shared experiences and histories, with actual presence, and with feedback loops designed to strengthen us. These five elements (closely associated with authenticity) make all the difference.

Why did the disciples trust Jesus? They were clearly not convinced beyond a shadow of a doubt about his divinity. They had their moments and questions along the way, even to the point of abandoning him at his trial and crucifixion. Yet, they trusted him enough to leave their work and families and follow him. Why? It's not hard to see our five "elements" played out in the Gospel stories. Jesus did not expect their total trust initially. He understood that trust builds gradually. He also knew it builds with consistency. He was not one thing when he was with them

> *One of the greatest challenges many leaders find is to delegate not just tasks but authority.*

and another when they weren't watching. He shared experiences and stories with them. They didn't pop into a seminar with him once a year. They lived and travelled with him every day. And he provided meaningful, candid, but caring feedback to them during the journey. He showed concern for their growth, and called them out graciously when they failed. Nobody ever said of Jesus: "He hates me!"

How do we produce more leaders? We work out our own security issues. We build trust with others and learn to trust them. Finally, we practice delegation. Ultimately, leadership must be given opportunity. It cannot be kept in mothballs. It must be put into practice, and delegation is a key element to releasing others.

3. Delegation

One of the greatest challenges many leaders find is the courage, capacity, and commitment to delegate — not just tasks, but authority. Yet, delegation lies at the heart of building not just a business, or a church, but the people.

Randall O'Brien, president of Carson-Newman College, wrote: "*Value, voice,* and *vote* are three good words for leaders to remember. All persons want to be valued, given voice, and allowed to participate in decision-making that affects them."[44] Yet, many leaders struggle to hand off responsibility to others.

In a counter-intuitive comment, Verne Harnish (writing for business leaders) says: "To get to 10 employees, founders must delegate activities in which they are weak. To get to 50 employees, they have to delegate functions in which they are strong! In many cases, the strength of the top leader becomes the weakness of the organization."[45]

We can identify various superficial reasons for not delegating to others. Quality control and time are two of the common excuses. "It won't be done as well as I like or as quickly as I need." But these things mask deeper issues. More commonly delegation is about control, insecurity, fear of failure, image, or the inability to manage people well. If you struggle with delegation, what are the real issues? Are you needing personal growth in this area? Or do you genuinely have the wrong people on the bus; people not ready to receive delegation? Either way, responsibility rests with you to make some changes to either yourself or your team.

Transformational leaders build the lives of others, and this requires (at a minimum) security, trust, and delegation. Are these firmly in place in your own leadership?

THE APPLETREE EXAMPLE

Appletree Answers employs 650 people and provides an answering service and call center based in Delaware, with satellite sites across the nation.

In 2008, executives at the company (which had expanded rather quickly and dramatically) found that they had a 110 percent turnover of employees who answered the phones for clients. This was a horrifyingly high turnover and John Ratliff, the founder, realized how out of touch his executive team had become with the call center workers.

The company had a stated core value, "Take care of each other" but it seemed meaningless. So, they launched an initiative—the Dream On initiative—and asked employees to submit a request for one thing they'd like to happen in their lives. The results were shocking.

Unbeknown to management, many employees were grappling with serious health issues. Others were trying to pay off crippling credit card debt from being unemployed before joining Appletree. Some hoped to buy a car so they could get to work (and home) more quickly without buses. One or two were actually homeless and living in their car! Ratliff began to listen to his workers and respond to some of their critical needs, getting genuinely involved in the lives of the employees.

Over a short period of time, the Dream On initiative had a profound impact on the turnover rate, which dropped to just 20 percent. While the initiative cost the company money (as they helped various employees with home rental deposits, utilities bills, etc.), it paid a 20 times return on investment in terms of reduced turnover costs *in less than a year.*

Furthermore, Appletree Answers re-shaped and re-stated its company Purpose to read: "Enhancing the lives of customers *and employees,* one interaction at a time."

John Ratliff is a transformational leader. And when he and his executive team began to care as much for their employees as for their customers, they found that the employee morale was higher, productivity increased, and annual profits grew. Win, win, win.

Research and widespread experience now shows that building lives is not just a nice idea. It's a winning strategy in leadership. When we realign our focus on the welfare and well-being of *all* people under our care and responsibility—clients, contractors, and kids alike—we advance both their lives and the organizational mission.

CHAPTER SUMMARY

Transformational leaders live with the constant awareness that their first calling is to produce change and build lives. They prioritize lives over products, and people over profits. They also grapple with the question, "How many people are flourishing under my leadership?" This focus on lives—whether it's the lives of employees or clients—requires leaders who are secure in their identity as human beings, who build trust with those around them, and who delegate authority (not just tasks) to others.

SOME POSSIBLE EXERCISES

Security

Ask two close friends or family members to describe ways you might express insecurity. Hear their feedback without defending yourself. Ponder it. Build it into your leadership roadmap for the next few weeks. Consider some meaningful next steps.

Trust

Meet with a leader you admire and discuss ways that they have built trust over the years. Which of their actions might be a helpful next step for you in your leadership?

Delegation

Rate yourself on a scale of 1 to 10 in terms of your ability or consistency (or both) in the art of delegation. What step might you take to move the needle closer to 10?

NOTES

Key thoughts you had while reading this chapter. **Questions** that came up. **Ideas** for personal next steps. **Insights** to discuss with a friend.

_____

_____

_____

_____

Chapter 4

Authenticity

"Control is not leadership; management is not leadership; leadership is leadership. If you seek to lead, invest at least 50 percent of your time in leading yourself — your own purpose, ethics, principles, motivation, and conduct." – Dee Hock

In May 2017, 26-year-old Oobah Butler decided to open a high-end restaurant in Dulwich, London. He called it The Shed. When it first opened, TripAdvisor — an online site where people leave comments about their experiences of hotels, restaurants, etc. — ranked The Shed dead last of the 14,189 restaurants in the London area. Five months later, in a meteoric rise to fame, the restaurant had climbed all the way to #1.

Would-be patrons to the restaurant had to call for reservations, but found that it was booked solid for months to come. The website featured a few photos of dishes, but no set menu. The chef would create masterpiece "mood food" based on how guests found themselves feeling on the evening.

But "contrary to the 100-plus raving TripAdvisor reviews that waxed poetic about the food's depth of flavor, the rustic décor, and a meal quite worth the wait, The Shed at Dulwich didn't actually exist."[46]

Butler, a freelance journalist had set up The Shed as a prank and a social experiment. With a little ingenuity, a burner cell-phone, a few friends, a fake website, and a large dose of mischief, he successfully created an entirely fake restaurant that became the talk of South London and generated 89,000 searches per day on TripAdvisor.

Some people "do leadership" with the same kind of smoke and mirrors as Oobah Butler. It's entirely possible to fool all of the people for some of the time and some of the people for all of the time. We see it every day. All it takes is the gift of the gab and plenty of confidence and enthusiasm. A firm handshake, rapid-fire talk, and loud volume overwhelms many a lesser soul. But this fake leadership eventually runs out of steam.

One of my favorite stories is Hans Christian Andersen's "*The Emperor's New Clothes*," first published in 1837. In the short story, two swindling weavers come to town and offer to make clothes from the finest cloth in human history for the vain Emperor. They warn everyone, however, that dolts and idiots would not be able to see the cloth, even when it was right in front of them.

Throughout the story, the swindlers proudly display the fabric they are weaving, but nobody — least of all the Emperor — is willing to say that the looms are empty, for fear of being branded a fool. Finally, the weavers finish the glorious new (non-existent) royal attire and the story finishes with these words:

> So off went the Emperor in procession under his splendid canopy. Everyone in the streets and the windows

said, "Oh, how fine are the Emperor's new clothes! Don't they fit him to perfection? And see his long train!" Nobody would confess that he couldn't see anything, for that would prove him either unfit for his position, or a fool. No costume the Emperor had worn before was ever such a complete success.

"But he hasn't got anything on," a little child said.

"Did you ever hear such innocent prattle?" said its father. And one person whispered to another what the child had said, "He hasn't anything on. A child says he hasn't anything on."

"But he hasn't got anything on!" the whole town cried out at last.

The Emperor shivered, for he suspected they were right. But he thought, "This procession has got to go on." So he walked more proudly than ever, as his noblemen held high the train that wasn't there at all.[47]

Many a leader has "walked more proudly than ever" despite the glaring truth about their lives, and many a follower has cow-towed to the fake and false leadership in front of them, for fear of looking foolish.

Authenticity is not as simple as we might imagine. Some authors have suggested that we "fake it till we make it." Herminia Ibarra's book *Act Like a Leader, Think Like a Leader* takes the counter-intuitive position that our thinking eventually catches up with our acting. Ibarra demonstrates that the more we do leadership (first) the more we begin to think like leaders (second).[48] She certainly makes valid assertions about confidence perhaps preceding competence, but authenticity (a character issue) rarely emerges from "faking it." John Lancaster Spalding was probably correct when he concluded that "the highest courage is to dare to appear to be what one is."

The renowned educator Parker Palmer wrote powerfully about a season in his life as a professor that lacked authenticity. In his own words:

> Schooled to speak and write, I used words in great volume for a number of years. Then came a time of dryness when I found it difficult to meet my classes, to speak in public, to write for publication or even for myself. That experience lasted for nearly two years. It made me desperate, angry, and despondent. I finally left my university career, convinced that conditions in the academy had caused my words to dry up.
>
> But now I see the deeper lesson my experience was meant to teach. Words began to fail me because I was not following them with my life. I was failing to incarnate what truth I had been given, and my words, lacking flesh, were skeletons with no animation or powers of regeneration. Only as I began to act on the social concerns I had spoken about in class, only as I began trying to live the vision of community I had once written about, did my words begin to return.[49]

Authenticity is like that. It makes us whole. It unites our words and our actions and thereby strengthens the soul. And while it serves to build our inner lives, it also serves as light to those whom we lead. It disempowers the darkness that prevails in so many businesses, churches, and homes. It connects us together.

Duplicity, on the other hand, does just the opposite. It fractures our inner lives. It confuses and disconnects those whom we would lead. It fosters suspicion and nurtures resentment.

Minorities in leadership (for example women, Hispanics, and African-Americans in a predominantly white male environment) face very real challenges in this area of *authenticity*. It's not that they are unwilling to be authentically themselves. Quite the contrary. They may crave to be as authentic as anyone in the organization. However, the organizational culture may so stereotype minorities that people from those groups feel forced to make accommodations that others do not. Hewlett has noted that:

> African-American women [in leadership] told us how carefully they step in order to tamp down the specter of the angry black woman, behavior that exacts a toll not only on their authenticity...but also on their productivity. Everyone we surveyed or spoke to affirmed the importance of authenticity, pointing out that no leader can win or retain followers without it. Everyone also agreed that succeeding in any organizational culture demands that you make accommodations to that culture.[50]

There are no simple or quick solutions to these challenges that minorities face. Ultimately, it requires an intentional effort on the part of those in positions of power. They simply must shape the culture of the church or the office to make authenticity increasingly safe and possible. Stereotypes and hidden biases[51] need to be identified, called out, and addressed.

Authenticity includes many different elements, but it surely includes at least these: Honesty and integrity, transparency, and humility.

HONESTY & INTEGRITY

Honesty and integrity are not skills to learn as a way to manipulate others. Rather, they have to do with the inner life and character of the leader. Ideally, they become deeply embedded within us and form our core—core values, core beliefs, and core commitments. We embrace them in smooth sailing and in stormy weather alike, because they represent not a leadership style but a cornerstone of our character.

Character is what we really are; reputation is what others think we are. The more that the two align, the greater our integrity. Indeed, perfect alignment is the essence of integrity and the course of great peace and strength.

> *Integrity implies that we live a single, integrated, and consistent life. The inside and the outside match up.*

Former Wyoming senator Alan Simpson once aid, "If you have integrity, nothing else matters. If you don't have integrity, nothing else matters."[52] While this is not entirely true—other aspects of leadership are also critically important—integrity is certainly at the top of a short list.

Integrity (from the same root as *integer,* meaning a whole number) implies that we live a single, integrated, and consistent life. The inside and the outside match up. What we are in private is essentially the same as what we show in public. And this consistency requires honesty.

Kroger CEO Dave Dillon likens integrity to a well-ordered traffic system. "You know that when the light is green, you can go, because people who want to go the other way are stopped at red. If you didn't have that [same level of faith and trust] in an organization, on every transaction you would have to start over."[53] Integrity produces that level of faith.

Honesty in leadership forms the bedrock for trust.

Leadership experts Jim Kouzes and Barry Posner have administered valuable leadership-related surveys for decades. After gathering data from over 75,000 people around the world, the same result came back year after year: honesty consistently ranks as the most desired leadership trait.[54]

Within transformational leaders, honesty manifests in two important ways. First, it relates to our speech. We speak with honesty. We say what we mean and mean what we say. Our word is our bond. If we say it, people can take it to the bank. Second, it relates to our actions. We model honesty and integrity in the way that we live. We exhibit consistency of character whether we say something specific or not. Our lives become open books and, to some extent, predictable for their consistency. People don't have to walk on eggshells around us, fearful of a sudden outburst or worried about unexpected hostility. Simon Sinek writes:

> When we suspect the leaders of a company are saying things to make themselves or the company look better than they are or to avoid humiliation or accountability, our trust in them falters. It is a natural response. Our brain interprets the information we receive with *our* survival in mind. If we suspect our leaders are bending the truth to favor their own interests, then our subconscious mind prefers we don't climb into a foxhole with them.[55]

In the 16th century, Machiavelli, renowned for his rather draconian political advice ("freeing political action from moral considerations"), believed that integrity leads only to defeat for leaders. In his view, theological and ethical considerations have no place in political life unless they serve a political purpose. He asked the question whether (as leaders) it is better to be loved or feared, and concluded: "The answer is, of course, that it would be best to be both loved and feared. But since the two rarely come together, anyone compelled to choose will find greater security in being feared than in being loved."[56] In his view, long-lasting leadership requires us to keep everyone off-balance, uncomfortable, and afraid. This minimizes any uprising that might prey on a gentle character.

As political advice, Machiavelli's *The Prince* has influenced countless leaders since its publication in 1532. But his political philosophy advocated tyrannical rule, not transformational leadership.

Jesus once famously said to some Jews who had decided to follow him: "If you hold to my teaching, you are really my disciples. Then you will know the truth, *and the truth will set you free*" (John 8:31-32).

> Any compromise of truth in our lives opens the door to distrust by others and inner dissonance.

Truth has that power. It sets us free, and the more consistently we live in truth, the more freedom we experience. Truth produces integrity (wholeness and authenticity), and it's not just truth when it's convenient, but truth when it's costly. It's not just truth about major issues, but truth in the smallest details. *Any* compromise of truth in our lives ("Tell them I'm not here") opens the door to some level of distrust and dissonance.[57]

Some leaders dismiss dishonesty and lying as mere political expediency or a necessary evil at times. They regard "white lies" as inconsequential, and generally draw a line only where legal consequences might come into play. Some don't draw a line even there. But this loose relationship with truth and honesty reflects a fundamental flaw, a deep inconsistency, and a brokenness within the leader.

We might lie or "stretch the truth" or "spin the facts" for any number of reasons. Sometimes we stand to gain from a cover-up. Other times we fear the consequences of truth. Perhaps we stand to lose something we want, or be forced to take a burdensome responsibility.

When Ben was a young man, he and a partner ran a small business that went bankrupt and left some investors deeply out of pocket. Ben's partner sought the protection of bankruptcy, but Ben committed to repaying every penny he had lost. He wouldn't lie, dodge, weave, or abdicate responsibility, though he spent decades making payments to fulfill his word and his pledge to those long-term creditors. When I met Ben, he was an older retired man with limited resources but with a magnetic warmth and a winsome integrity about him, and people looked to him as a leader.

Transformational leadership, whether in the home or the office, rises and falls with integrity. We simply must not compromise that integrity. We should guard it like a lion guards its den. But beyond honesty and integrity, we might consider another hallmark of authenticity: Transparency.

TRANSPARENCY

Some people consider transparency to be dangerous, particularly those folk who think leaders should keep their distance and keep their secrets. They fear that too much transparency could undermine respect. They assume that if leaders are too open about their own lives or about the reality of the organization, the team members might lose confidence. "Familiarity breeds contempt."

Research, however, increasingly finds that transparency is vital to building a culture (or family) of trust. It is core to a lifestyle of authenticity. Andre Lavoie noted in 2015:

> Believe it or not, a full quarter of employees don't trust their employer, according to a 2014 American Psychological Association survey of 1,562 U.S. workers. What's more, the survey also found that only about half believe their employer is open and upfront with them.[58]

This perceived lack of transparency undermines both confidence and trust within an organization. When people sense that their leaders are hiding layers beneath layers within an organization, they tend to either isolate or leave. Silos form quickly in the absence of transparency. It's a natural protective mechanism. Since knowledge is power, we tend to fear hidden knowledge and either retreat into our own corners (where we have full knowledge) or depart to new pastures (where we hope to experience a more open and collaborative environment).

Transparency does not apply only to small or simple organizations. Incredibly complex organizations can still function with transparency. Indeed, many companies have proprietary knowledge about products and prototypes and I'm not suggesting for a moment that such information be laid bare for all employees or the world to see. Transparency is not about endangering company viability or security. It relates instead to shaping a less political culture within the workplace.

Unbounce is a Canadian software company based in Vancouver, BC. It took transparency to another level with its "Inside Unbounce" blog, a staff-authored, un-curated window to the organization.[59] This raw blog, written by employees for employees, models transparency to potential job seekers and customers, and keeps employees involved and current on company happenings, successes and feedback.

HubSpot, another major developer and marketer of software products, puts transparency at the top of its Culture Code. The company has an internal wiki that includes its financial data (cash balances, burn-rate, profits and losses, etc.), board meeting info, strategic topics, HubSpot Lore & Mythology, and more; all to help employees stay informed and aligned with the company vision.[60]

LinkedIn CEO Jeff Weiner also fosters an organization built on transparency. He frequently takes time to hold bi-weekly meetings, during which he updates employees on company matters and listens to their suggestions.

These tech industry companies are leading the way in organizational (and transformational) leadership. Their workplace practices sound radical and leave some people nervous. "Yes, but what if...?" What if people get out of their lanes? What if people don't handle information well? Yet, these practices simply reflect the ancient conviction that openness and transparency provides a much surer pathway to strong relationships, greater collaboration, increased cohesion, and collective freedom.

Theologians and pastors have recognized for centuries that secrecy empowers sin. Secrecy encourages darkness. It covers up the light. It hides the truth. It conceals reality, and it threatens the stability of communities.

In Acts 19 we read about the apostle Paul traveling to the ancient city of Ephesus. In a dramatic incident, some Jewish exorcists were overpowered by a demon-possessed man and fear spread among the local people who were renowned in the ancient world for their practice of magic. We read: "Many of those who believed now came and openly confessed what they had done. A number who had practiced sorcery brought their [expensive] scrolls together and burned them publicly" (Acts 19:18-19). What was happening in that moment? The confession was not simply an admission that they had practiced the dark arts. The entire community knew that already. Rather, it seems far more likely that their confession involved actually pronouncing out loud the incantations and spells, thereby breaking the secrecy and power that had held people and the community in bondage for far too long.

Any of us who have carried a deep or dark secret within us know the insidious impact it has on the soul, particularly over time. The longer we carry it, the stronger its grip usually becomes, and the more difficult it can be to expose it to the light. Transparency is the solution for this darkness. Transparency liberates the captive soul, and we see this reflected even in modern psychology.

Twelve Step recovery programs insist on transparency. Alcoholics Anonymous (AA), founded by Bill Wilson, originated the idea for the Twelve Step model in 1938. Since then, many spin-off programs have emerged but the steps remain fundamentally consistent. Each one begins with the same step; admitting the addiction and one's own powerlessness over it.[61]

Similarly, psychologists see many people who suffer from post-traumatic stress disorder (PTSD). This commonly occurs when a person witnesses or experiences a particularly threatening or frightening ordeal. Military veterans and first-responders (police, fire, and ambulance) can experience it, but so can victims of violent crime or abuse.

The stress often manifests through insomnia, flashbacks, low self-esteem, and a lot of painful and unpleasant emotions. But the treatment protocol is uniformly the same: psychotherapy and medication. In the psychotherapy, clients discuss the event with a therapist and may even write it out in considerable detail. They become transparent about it. Without this initial step, medication serves only to mask the malady, not to heal the heart.

> *There's a difference between discretion and deceit.*

Transparency, then, is not just a leadership principle but a life principle, and transformational leaders embrace this intentionally and strategically as part of their leadership philosophy.

There are obviously those times when we deliver the truth over time, not all in one moment. To quote the famous line of Jack Nicholson when being interrogated by Tom Cruise in the 1992 American legal thriller *A Few Good Men*, "You can't handle the truth!" But there's a difference between distorting the truth, concealing the truth, and delivering the truth in manageable pieces. There's a world of difference between discretion, done with the group's welfare in mind, and deceit, undertaken to protect individual interest.

Transparency, as an element of authenticity, does not require that we tell everything to everyone. That might be both unwise and unfair. But transparency is a commitment to openness and inclusiveness. Ultimately, buy-in from our teams (and our spouses, if we apply this to marriage) becomes greatest when people feel trusted and included, rather than marginalized and side-lined.

We demonstrate real authenticity through honesty, integrity, and transparency. But a final feature that proves core to authenticity is humility.

HUMILITY

In the days of stagecoaches, outlaws, and the Wild West, you had choices. When you bought a ticket on the nine-passenger Concord stagecoach, you could choose between three options.

First-class tickets guaranteed you a seat in the coach no matter what the weather or circumstances, though you might still be robbed or shot. Second-class tickets required you to get out of the coach from time to time and walk alongside it, if the horses were tired or the road too muddy to allow easy passage. Third-class tickets—the cheapest—allowed you to ride in the coach but required you to get out, roll up your sleeves, and push it when it was bogged or negotiating particularly steep terrain...*and do so without complaining.*

No prizes for guessing what ticket transformational leaders purchase when they say "Yes" to leadership. Or is that not so obvious?

In a culture steeped in entitlement, a culture that expects leadership to involve perks and privileges, and a culture that believes leaders have a more sacred role than followers, we may actually (perhaps even unintentionally) start believing that leaders are first-class ticket-holders.

But the kingdom of God, in typical fashion, turns such wrong-headed thinking upside down. The decision to follow Jesus is also a commitment to *"get out and push whenever asked – without complaining."*

Upon her inauguration as president at the then-beleaguered and struggling Vanguard University (Southern California) in 2010, Carol Taylor received a Third-Class Ticket. The speaker in that service – Dr. George Wood – made it clear that the presidency was not a pathway to privilege but the responsibility to serve sacrificially, whole-heartedly, and uncomplainingly.[62] Taylor took it to heart and went on to lead the university through a remarkable cultural and financial turnaround over the next few years.

Grumbling and complaining can reach sophisticated levels among leaders, who might like to look like martyrs without shedding a drop of blood. But a chronic "Woe is me" attitude perhaps betrays a "first-class ticket" heart, and something less than the humility that underscores authentic leadership.

Transformational leadership is built on third-class tickets, not first-class tickets.

In a renowned 2011 Harvard Business Review article, Jim Collins described what he called "Level 5 Leadership." It's the top-level leadership that distinguishes great leaders from merely good leaders. This category of Level 5 leadership emerged from Collins' analysis of 1,435 successful companies, only eleven of which he described as truly great and headed by Level 5 leaders.

Here, according to Collins, are the hallmarks (in order) of those Level 5 leaders.

- ❖ They have humility.
- ❖ They don't seek success for their own glory.
- ❖ They share credit for success.
- ❖ They are the first to accept blame for mistakes.
- ❖ They may be shy but they're fearless when it comes to making decisions.

> *Humility was the outstanding trait in the best of the best.*

These Level 5 leaders exhibit many qualities and traits of leadership, but humility was the outstanding trait in the best of the best.[63] In the list above, the second, third, and fourth characteristics that Collins identified, really define humility as well.

Johannes Brahms, the nineteenth century German composer, enjoyed great popularity. On one occasion he met an ardent music lover who asked, "Master, would you please write here a small portion of a masterpiece and sign it so I can have a precious memory of this fortunate encounter?" Brahms took the pencil and paper offered to him, scribbled the initial few bars of *The Blue Danube* (composed by one of his contemporaries, Johann Strauss) and signed: "Unfortunately not by me, Johannes Brahms."

Transformational leaders do not seek glory for themselves. They do not lead in order to build their own resumes. They deflect credit to others which, ironically, tends to come back to them anyway. And they take responsibility for mistakes.

Of course, we can all think of leaders who exhibit just the opposite. They model self-interest and self-aggrandizement. They want (and seem to need) credit for every small achievement. They refuse to accept responsibility for mistakes or failures. Indeed, they may refuse to ever apologize. They have convinced themselves that they're above most people and they wield power with coercion and intimidation. This is a form of leadership, but it's not transformational leadership. It generally breeds insecurity in others and instability in the workplace or the organization. People know that they must yield and do obeisance or face difficult consequences. Ultimately, it produces environments of paranoia and isolation.

Humility, on the other hand, has sometimes been misinterpreted as weakness. The common wisdom suggests that people take advantage of humble leaders, and humble leaders sacrifice their careers on the altar of niceness and conflict-avoidance. Nothing could be further from the truth.

Humility has been defined by some people as "not thinking less of yourself, but thinking of yourself less." It's a profoundly important distinction, and the quintessential biblical example is provided by the apostle Paul in Philippians 2:3-8.

Do nothing out of selfish ambition or vain conceit. Rather, in humility value others above yourselves, not looking to your own interests but each of you to the interests of others.

In your relationships with one another, have the same mindset as Christ Jesus, who, being in very nature God did not consider equality with God something to be used to his own advantage; rather, he made himself nothing by taking the very nature of a servant, being made in human likeness. And being found in appearance as a man, he humbled himself by becoming obedient to death — even death on a cross!

This exhortation urges us to embrace lives of self-emptying humility in every area, including leadership. Furthermore, it highlights the enormous strength, resolve, courage, and character required to choose this path. Humility is not for the weakest but for the strongest of leaders. We may have little control

> *Humility is not for the weakest but for the strongest.*

over humiliation that comes our way, but authentic humility is absolutely a matter of choice, and it undergirds authentic transformational leadership in deep and powerful ways.

Do you recognize the name Irena Sendler? She was one of the world's truly transformational leaders. In 1983 the Israeli Supreme Court confirmed her as one of the *Righteous Among the Nations*.[64] In 2003 she received a personal letter of commendation from Pope John Paul II and Poland's highest civilian decoration, the *Order of the White Eagle*. In 2007 she was nominated for the *Nobel Peace Prize*. She eventually died on May 12, 2008 at 98 years of age, though relatively few of us know her inspiring story.

Born in Poland, Irena Sendler joined the Polish Zegota resistance movement that opposed the Nazis during World War II. Along with some two dozen other Zegota members, Sendler saved 2,500 Jewish children from the Warsaw Ghetto. She would enter the Ghetto as a Nazi-approved social worker to check for signs of typhus, then conceal small children in boxes, suitcases, and trolleys and smuggle them out of the Ghetto. Outside, she provided the children with false documents and sheltered them in safe places.

Remarkably, Irena Sendler herself was not a Jew.

In 1943, the Gestapo arrested Sendler, tortured her, and sentenced her to death. Members of the Zegota saved her by bribing German guards on the way to her execution. She spent the remainder of the war in hiding.

During her smuggling activities, she made lists of both the real names and the new identities of the children, in the hope that after the war she might be able to reunite them with their families. She hid these lists of names in jars that she buried, though after the war she found that almost all of the parents had perished at the Treblinka extermination camp or gone missing.

This quiet, humble woman sought no glory. She did not consider her efforts to be heroic. Reflecting on her work with and for Jewish children, she once said, "Every child saved with my help...is the justification of my existence on this earth, *and not a title to glory.*"

Her life stands as a stark contrast to the glory-seeking, attention-grabbing, self-asserting ways of our day. She had the humble heart of a transformational servant.

Dan Allender has given considerable thought to this topic of humility (as many have) and concluded:

> No one is humble by nature.... Humility comes from humiliation, not from the choice to be self-effacing or a strong urge to give others credit. Humility that has not come from suffering due to one's own arrogance is either a pragmatic strategy to get along with others or a natural predilection that seems to befit only a few rare individuals. For most leaders, humility comes only by wounds suffered from foolish falls. This is the terrible secret about leadership and life: we achieve brokenness by falling off our throne.[65]

Allender is partly right. Failure and humiliation can certainly humble us, and our wounds can certainly change our perspective in profound ways. However, brokenness does not guarantee humility, and pain does not ensure change. We see far too many leaders leave a trail of damage in their wake, first in one place and then the next because of unhealed wounds and unresolved hurts. At some point, broken or not, humility is a choice.

> *Brokenness does not guarantee humility, and pain does not ensure change. Humility is a choice.*

Thus, transformational leadership starts with authenticity. We talk the talk *and* walk the walk. We don't tell; we show. And with each step towards greater authenticity, we take a step towards more effective leadership. This authenticity emerges from a deep and consistent commitment to honesty, integrity, transparency, and humility.

Think of the most influential spiritual mentor in your life? Is it the person who *knew* the most Scripture, or the one who *lived* the most Scripture? Similarly, think of your most effective mentor in general, if you've experienced one. Did you warm to the person with the most information, or someone whose experience and character formed a unified whole and whose integrity and authenticity resonated with you?

CHAPTER SUMMARY

Transformational leaders embrace authenticity. They are consistently the same person in public as in private. They practice honesty and integrity at *all* times, and live with a high degree of transparency. They don't need to keep secrets, nor do they live double-lives. This authenticity also manifests in humility. Transformational leaders do not need the limelight nor do they steal credit from others. They lead with enormous determination but not with enormous self-centeredness. They devote themselves to the cause (family, church, or business) and to building others, without much thought about "What's in this for me?" Their authenticity builds their credibility in the eyes of others, as it makes them approachable and reliable. It also makes the leader a whole and unified individual.

SOME POSSIBLE EXERCISES

Honesty & Integrity

In five minutes, finish this sentence "Truth matters because..." with as many ideas or thoughts as possible. Put your top five insights onto a 3 x 5 card (something physical, not electronic) and carry it with you in your car for the next 14 days, so you can ponder it longer and more deeply.

Transparency

Identify two people with whom you could be a little more transparent this week. Find ways to share more with them; what you're going through, how you're feeling, and what you're thinking. How does this affect those relationships?

Humility

Do something this week to serve someone without anyone knowing it was you. Process the experience. How did it feel? What did you discover?

NOTES

Key thoughts you had while reading this chapter. **Questions** that came up. **Ideas** for personal next steps. **Insights** to discuss with a friend.

_____

_____

_____

_____

_____

Chapter 5

Inspiration

"If your actions inspire others to dream more, learn more, do more, and become more, you are a leader." – John Quincy Adams

Transformational leadership inspires others. It's more than plain hard work. It casts a vision and motivates people towards a preferred future.

Henry Ford revolutionized the western world when he began to mass-produce automobiles for the common people. He didn't invent the automobile or the assembly-line, but he did produce vehicles that middle-class Americans could afford.

The first Model T Ford rolled off the assembly-line on October 1, 1908 priced at $825. By 1916, the price for the basic model had dropped to $360 and Ford was dominating the market in a way that nobody could have imagined. By 1918, half of all cars in America were black Model T's (the only color available) and when production of the Model T stopped in 1927 (19 years after the launch), over 15 million vehicles had been sold – a record that stood for the next 45 years.

Ford's ingenuity and dedication has inspired mechanics and magnates ever since. On one occasion, Ford said:

"Whether you think you can or you think you can't, you're right."

Transformational leaders inspire people to think they can, but inspiration is not simply about producing a wow-factor. We often feel inspired after attending a performance of Handel's *Messiah* or watching people overcome great odds to achieve impressive goals in life. I've always marveled at the incredible story of the Hoyts.

Richard "Dick" Hoyt is the father of Richard Jr. "Rick" Hoyt. Rick was born on January 10, 1962 with cerebral palsy and has been confined to a wheelchair his whole life. But in 1977, Rick asked his dad if they could run in a race together to benefit a friend at school who had been paralyzed. And thus began Team Hoyt.

Dick was 36 years old and was not a runner. But the father and son duo began entering various athletic competitions together. If it involved swimming, Dick would pull Rick in a little boat. If it included cycling, Rick would sit in a special seat on the front of the bicycle. And during runs, Dick would push Rick in a custom-made wheelchair.

From 1977 to their retirement together in 2016 (yes, nearly 40 years), they competed together in 1,130 endurance events, including 72 marathons and seven Ironman triathlons. They ran the Boston Marathon 32 times and also biked across the United States in 1992, completing the 3,735 miles in just 45 days. They were inducted into the Ironman Hall of Fame in 2008, and a bronze statue in their honor was dedicated on April 8, 2013 near the start of the Boston Marathon in Hopkinton, Massachusetts.

That kind of resilience, courage, and story is truly moving. Those two men have defied the odds together and done more than most of us can imagine. But it doesn't necessarily motivate us to action. You're not likely to put this book down right now, throw on some shoes, and start a mind-boggling running career with someone who's disabled. So, when we talk about inspiration, there's something deeper than the wow-factor or the feeling of wonder.

MISTAKEN INSPIRATION

We often make some simple mistakes when we try to inspire and motivate other people.

First, we might assume that what motivates *us* will surely motivate *others*. For example, if we get charged up by sporting analogies and metaphors, we might assume everyone feels the same way. We might start speaking about ourselves in football terms, calling team-members running backs, blockers, receivers, punters, or special team players. Of course, in our minds, we're the quarterback calling all of the plays. This *cohesion tactic*—a way to connect everybody—might be effective in some small circles, but when it comes to inspiration, one size and one approach generally does not fit everyone.

Second, we may fail to link the vision of the future with anything of value to the individual. We see this all the time and many churches are notorious for it. For example, pastors will exhort congregants to bring friends and neighbors to church services. "Let's see if we can get 400 (or 1,000 or 5,000) people here for Christmas." But this has little specific value to the person in the pew. Elders and pastors may like it from an image or reputation perspective, but there's no intrinsic value for the average person. So, despite the hard push from the platform, there's relatively little interest from church members. They intuitively know that a crowd of 500 or 5,000 will not add anything of great significance to their own lives or their own Christmas experience. The big crowd does not enhance the individual experience very much, if at all. Consequently, in most instances, it's less than inspiring and relatively few people get on board with the "vision." Some folk, in smaller churches may join the recruiting drive because of guilt or shame, but that's not the fruit of vision-casting.

Third, we can forget that our personal goals do not usually make good corporate goals. Many leaders know that certain achievements will look good on their resume and enhance their personal career prospects (new products, higher sales, larger staff, bigger budgets) but this may not motivate other team-members. Even when the team leader is well-liked by their team members, there's a limit (usually fairly low and reached fairly quickly) to what others are willing to do to support us. The *personal appeal* is a well that we cannot return to too often.

Transformational leadership provides inspirational motivation, but it's the inspiration that leads other people to see value and purpose for both the organization *and themselves*, in what they're doing. Interestingly, most people measure this value in terms other than money.

VISION CASTING
In light of these common mistakes, it should be clear that successful vision casting—one element of inspiration—

involves using common language; something that resonates with all team members. It includes identifying the value and significance for each individual team member as well as the organization, and a sense that this is not all about one person (specifically, the reputation of the leader).

Vision is to a family or organization what a melody line is to music. Harmonization in music allows people or instruments to move up and down throughout a basic melody line. For example, four-part and barber-shop quartet music, may have very different harmonies at work simultaneously, but the entire piece is held together by one controlling melody line. Healthy (and helpful) vision within an organization functions in much the same way.

When people embrace a common language, feel personal value, and believe that the vision is for the whole organization (and beyond), they more readily jump onboard.

For the record, many organizations have vision statements that aren't worth the paper they're written on, much less the time they took to devise. Many vision statements are too unrealistic ("change the world"), too abstract ("add value to people's lives"), too complex (lengthy paragraphs that look like the work of a conflicted committee), and therefore too forgettable. This largely undermines any inspirational value they may have had.

I agree with Verne Harnish that vision statements (faddish for a time) have fallen from grace because they were rarely done well or done right. It's better not to have a vision statement, than to have a meaningless one. It's probably better (and more useful) to have a clear mission statement. So, don't assume that a vision statement will inspire everyone and become the common language of the organization just because it is printed and posted in bathroom stalls.

Here's a tip. If you want a vision statement, remember that vision involves "seeing." A vision "statement" should be framed in terms of something your team can see. For example, "No child left behind" is far stronger than "Every child gets a good education." Or Microsoft's ambitious vision in its early days — "A computer in every home" — was surely better than "Quality electronics for the future." Yes, these images are captured as slogans, catch-phrases, tag-lines, or mottos. Call them what you will, but the vision of an organization must be catchable and memorable.

You might consider replacing the classic vision statement with a vision *story*. Harvard scholar Howard Gardner wrote, "Leaders achieve their effectiveness through the stories they relate."[66] Other scholars have noted the power of a genesis story (where this all began) for many organizations and movements. Even families find themselves bonded by their genesis stories. How did mom and dad meet? What happened in the early years? What family experiences reflect our core values? And so on.

> Consider replacing the classic vision statement with a vision story.

William Jessup University has, as part of its vision, a "genesis story" associated with the founder, William (Bill) Jessup. Early in the history of the University, when finances were especially tight, Brother Bill (as many knew him) called the faculty together. The cash flow of the University — a very small Bible College at the time — was all in a cardboard shoebox. There was no money for salary checks. Bill Jessup picked up the box and passed it around, urging faculty to take what they truly needed for their families. Brother Bill himself was the last to get the box. The story has reminded generations of faculty of the passion and calling that has sustained the University, and calls current faculty to similar passion, calling, and faithfulness to our roots (though the cardboard box has long since disappeared).

A congregation in southern California adopted the following story as their vision story, which they told repeatedly and wove deeply into the DNA of their church.

A young boy went down to the beach after a massive storm had swept through. The beach was littered with tens of thousands of starfish. The boy started to pick them up one at a time and throw them back into the water. An older man came along and asked the boy, "What are you doing?" "Saving starfish," the boy replied. "Saving starfish?" the man said. "But there are so many...too many. It won't make any difference." The boy bent down and picked up another starfish and tossed it into the water. "Made a difference to that one."

Stories have tremendous power. A punchline can catch us off guard, and in doing so drive home a memorable message. Good stories also typically have multiple unspoken layers that make them remarkably diverse in application. Furthermore, a good story tends to lodge in a different part of the brain than mathematical formulae. It grips our imagination and stirs our creativity in a way that Pythagoras' Theorem[67] (as true as it is) rarely does.

Vision matters, but *how high* we cast a vision matters more. Les Brown once quipped: "We don't fail because we aim too high and miss; we fail because we aim too low and hit." So, transformational leaders aim high and call people to a higher (and better) place. Truly transformational leaders demonstrate both authentic optimism and realism. Hope and a high vision is their calling card.

Vision matters, but *how often* we cast a vision matters more. As Margaret Carty playfully noted: "Be like a postage stamp: stick to one thing until you get there." Visioneering is not what you do annually at a staff retreat or semi-annually in a planning meeting. It oozes into conversations, meetings, and marketing, all the time. After analyzing countless organizations, John Kotter suggests that many organizations undercommunicate their vision by a factor of 10, 100, or even 1,000.[68]

> *Hope and a high vision is the calling card of truly transformational leaders.*

Vision matters, but *how relevant* we make a vision matters more. If the vision doesn't produce guidance, focus, inspiration, and value to everyone connected with it, it's probably deficient. It should guide our decision-making, help us to decide which opportunities to pursue and which to decline, inspire us with something bigger than ourselves, and have measurable value for everyone involved (the staff, the customer, and the community).

We could explore much more with regards to vision, but if you can avoid these few common mistakes and implement these few core components, you'll be well ahead of most organizations. And, once again, this has as much relevance to parenting and other leadership contexts, as to organizational presidency.

HALLMARKS OF INSPIRATION

Vision casting is but one tool for inspiring others. Inspiration builds on a number of other factors, too. Consider these three hallmarks of inspiration: Clarification, compensation, and celebration.

Clarification. Transformational leaders inspire others by clarifying or contextualizing what's going on. The old saying reminds us: "Don't overestimate what can be done in the short-term or underestimate what can be done in the long-term." Very often, transformational leaders are not simply pointing to the distant future, but inspiring their followers by helping them maintain perspective in the present.

Oprah Winfrey once told an audience: "If you look at what you have in life, you'll always have more. If you look at what you don't have in life, you'll never have enough." She simply reminded people that perspective makes a profound difference. If you adopt one perspective you'll be content and grateful. If you adopt the other perspective you'll more likely be discontent and greedy.

The late W. Edwards Deming put a slightly different spin on clarification. He suggested that "the fundamental job of a leader is prediction." This *prediction* (if it's to be accurate and helpful) requires more than an innate or uncanny sense of the future. It often emerges from good data analysis and market awareness. But ultimately, good *prediction* serves to provide *clarification* for others on the team. And it's this clarification that inspires and motivates people.

If clarification inspires, then confusion demotivates. This is no more readily apparent than in homes and families. Children who grow up with stability, predictability, security, boundaries, and routine generally do better as adults. Are there regular exceptions? Of course. But households marked by bickering, bitterness, chaos, and confusion are less than inspiring to many children. If we want to inspire our kids, we must clarify pathways and possibilities for them. We must remind them that a "C" in math is not the end of the world, that moving homes or schools will be OK, or that the death of a Christian loved one still has hope associated with it.

This is what transformational leaders do. They clarify and contextualize the circumstances for those around them. On the flip-side we might also note that while sometimes we have to say "It's not as bad as you think," there may be occasions when leaders have to say "It's *worse* than you think!"

Think about the family context again for a moment. Contextualizing for parents might mean settling down an over-stressed child or teen, helping them realize that this experience is not the end of the world. But it might equally mean on occasion, helping our children grasp the seriousness of their actions and perhaps the pain or hurt that they have caused others. This *clarification* is what leads to change and ultimately better lives.

Inspiration, then, involves both vision-casting and clarification. In the workplace it is also often connected with compensation.

Compensation. People are not always moved first and foremost by their paycheck, but compensation matters. At some point, perhaps a different point for each person (depending on their life stage and circumstance) the financial cost of remaining with an organization over-rides their commitment to the mission. This tipping point varies, but everyone has one, unless they are basically retired and willing to work and serve at their own expense. While money does not always inspire people beyond the moment, lack of monetary benefit can become very demotivating.

Psychologists tell us that money is one of the leading causes of marital conflict; the lack of it, or choices about how to divide it or spend it.[69] Little wonder then, that this domestic pressure rolls into the workplace at times.

A famous 2010 Princeton study found that well-being rose with income, but not much beyond $75,000 per year (at that time).[70] Conversely, incomes below $50,000 put increasing stress on relationships and families. The numbers obviously need to be adjusted from one region to another and over time. $50,000 in New York City will spend quite differently than in Waco, Texas. But we should not miss the point. There are thresholds below which dissatisfaction is high and above which satisfaction increases in only the smallest increments. Remuneration and inspiration indeed have a correlation.

Transformational leaders know that inspiration is about more than just words. Some Chick-Fil-A franchises start their workers at $1.50 above minimum wage and build in semi-annual reviews with the opportunity for small pay bumps at each review. For young people just entering the workforce, this can be inspiring. "Good job!" is encouraging to hear, but a stronger financial safety net makes all the difference when a baby's on the way, the rent rises, or the car breaks down.

In 2018, Eric Mason, a Sacramento Chick-Fil-A franchise owner (remember, this is fast food!) hit national news when he announced that from June 1 that year, all of his workers would earn at least $17 per hour (55 percent above the State mandated minimum wage) so they could have a "living wage."[71] Needless to say, his team of "hospitality professionals" felt appreciated, motivated, and inspired.

Celebration. Transformational leaders understand that inspiration and celebration are also linked. However, we might note quickly that celebration takes varied forms. Some people warm well to public recognition; others prefer private affirmation. Some people get inspired by awards or perks; others prefer promotion. Celebration takes many shapes, but organizations frequently overlook the significance of it.

Jimmy Calano, who built CareerTrack Inc. into the largest one-day-seminar company in the world, asked managers each month to submit three ideas for increasing revenue, reducing costs, or making something easier within the company. Then he would choose the top ideas for the month, announce them at a management meeting, and hand each winner a crisp $20 bill for fun. In some companies, leaders take half a dozen workers to dinner at one of the area's best restaurants each month to celebrate achievements.

> *Inspiration flourishes amidst celebration.*

In the corporate culture of America, we rarely stop to celebrate. More often than not, we finish one project, shoot a quick email to thank the team for their effort, and rush straight on to the next effort. We may even overlap projects and programs so there's no natural space to pause, acknowledge, and celebrate a win. As always, that can be true of business, churches, and families. Yet, inspiration flourishes in places where there is also celebration. Families and companies thrive when they celebrate, honor, and laugh together.

Leadership theorists James Kouzes and Barry Posner have found the same thing. They have identified what they call "*The Five Practices of Exemplary Leadership.*" Tested by hundreds of scholars in a wide range of settings, including leadership in religious organizations, their fifth practice is "Encourage the Heart." According to Kouzes and Posner this involves at least two steps. First, recognize contributions by showing appreciation for individual excellence. Second, celebrate the values and victories of the team by creating a spirit of community.[72]

In a similar vein, change guru John Kotter has concluded that a strategic step in making long-term change is to create and celebrate short-term wins. He writes: "Little wins offer an opportunity to relax for a few minutes and celebrate. Constant tension for long periods of time is not healthy for people. The little celebration following a win can be good for the body and spirit.[73]

Celebrate. It matters!

I've always liked the simple reminder provided by the consonants in the word "PRAISE." Praise is best when it is Personal, Random, and Specific. It's nice to say "You are all amazing!" but it's better to say "Karen, you brought wonderful creativity to that project!" Make it Personal. But praise has additional power when it comes unexpectedly. A business awards night is fine, but unexpected honor is better. Catching someone mid-way through a project, when they least expect it, is far more affirming. Make it Random. Finally, to say to someone "We really appreciate you" is thoughtful, but to say "You showed great wisdom and grace in handling that particular student" touches a deeper place. Make it Specific.

These principles associated with inspiration—vision-casting, clarification, compensation, and celebration—have a long history. These are not 21st century developments. Indeed, we find them even in the life and ministry of Jesus.

INSPIRATION IN THE LIFE OF JESUS

As Jesus announced the arrival of the kingdom of God, he regularly used stories, similes, and metaphors to describe it. At times he described how the kingdom would function and how people would act within it. His famous Sermon on the Mount (Matthew 5-7) describes kingdom life in extraordinary terms. But on other occasions he used parables and pictures. For example, the kingdom of heaven is like a mustard seed, like leaven, like a treasure hidden in a field, like a merchant seeking fine pearls, like a dragnet (Matthew 13:31, 33, 44, 45, 47).

Jesus also did something very powerful with code language. Historically, revolutionaries and change agents have used insider language to inspire their followers and disguise their rhetoric from the general populace or ruling authorities. Jesus did this same thing by describing himself regularly as the "Son of Man."[74] To Roman or Gentile ears (perhaps even to our own), this phrase sounds innocent and generic; a declaration that Jesus is "just another guy" more or less. But to insiders, this phrase carried deep and inspiring meaning. The connection with Daniel 7:13-14 (itself a subversive book) was unmistakable. Daniel wrote:

I kept looking in the night visions, and behold, with the clouds of heaven one *like a Son of Man* was coming, and he came up to the Ancient of Days and was presented before him. And to him was given dominion, glory and a kingdom that all the peoples, nations and men of every language might serve him. His dominion is an everlasting dominion which will not pass away; and his kingdom is one which will not be destroyed.

In Daniel's prophecy—which was very familiar to any Jewish audience in the first century—the Son of Man is a glorious savior-figure whom the Ancient of Days (God himself) appoints as king. Indeed, God grants the *Son of Man* dominion, glory, and an eternal kingdom. That kind of language will rally the troops!

The apostle Paul does a similar thing with his use of the word "gospel." To most of us, the word simply means "good news" (a literal translation of the original Greek word). But Paul, as a revolutionary, has picked up an enormously powerful word and uses it to inspire his readers and hearers.

When Paul uses the Greek word *euangellion* ("good news/gospel") and tells his readers that he is set apart for this gospel (Romans 1:1) and is eager to preach it in Rome (Romans 1:15) and is not ashamed of it (Romans 1:16), he taps into something with rich history.

Before the first century, the Jews used the word "gospel" to describe the time when God would inaugurate his kingdom in a new way—a new kingdom, a new age, a new king, a fresh start (e.g. Isaiah 61:1). To the Jews "gospel" was a deeply social, political, theological, and spiritual term. It was very exciting. God was breaking in!

The Romans also used the word "gospel." However, they used it to describe the birth of their Emperor, or the Emperor's successful return from battle. To the Romans, "gospel" was a deeply political term as well.

But then Paul absconds with the word. He lifts it from the usual Jewish and Roman context and imbues it with new meaning; deep, powerful meaning. And it inspires people. It taps into their deepest longings, greatest needs, and fondest hopes.

The launch of any new cause requires inspirational language or the launch will splutter at best. The early believers and followers of Jesus knew this well. They seized upon common terms, commandeered them, refined them or redefined them, and cast a powerful and compelling subversive message right under the noses of the occupying forces.

Many leadership books, courses, and seminars identify inspiration as core to the leadership enterprise, and they are right to do so. But inspiration is more than good salesmanship, and much more than dumping an avalanche of information. It involves the nuanced art of vision-casting, and the consistent practice of clarification, compensation, and celebration.

CHAPTER SUMMARY

Leadership always involves inspiration. We only follow those who can show us a better way. But transformational leaders inspire us with some very simple practices. First, they cast vision that we can actually see, often using stories rather than statements. Then they inspire by providing clarification, compensation, and celebration. These simple tools distinguish transformational leaders from gate-keepers. They help us keep perspective in challenging times (clarification). They understand that we all have a tipping point when dedication to a cause or a company can no longer be sustained because the compensation is inadequate. And they take time to celebrate achievements and wins, rather than rush endlessly from one project to the next without recognition of success. Transformational leaders inspire others and regularly refine the art of inspiration.

SOME POSSIBLE EXERCISES

Vision Casting

What vision do you have for your marriage, family, church, or workplace? Describe it in terms that people can "see" not simply "understand." What picture or story best describes how things might look two years from now?

Clarification

Identify two points of particular stress for yourself right now. Do an exercise in clarification. Is this stress reasonable? Is it based on fact or fear? What simple *and previously unconsidered steps* might you take to better handle the concern?

Compensation

Make a list of ways you might better compensate those whom you lead, bearing in mind that financial compensation is just one possibility. What "rewards" would your people (even your spouse or your children) best respond to? Try it out!

Celebration

If you tend not to stop and celebrate much, surprise your family, your team, or your congregation with something celebratory—a special meal, donuts, balloons, afternoon tea, fun awards, public story-telling and praise, unexpected time off, etc. How did you feel? How do you think others felt?

NOTES

Key thoughts you had while reading this chapter. **Questions** that came up. **Ideas** for personal next steps. **Insights** to discuss with a friend.

_____

_____

_____

_____

_____

_____

Chapter 6

Empathy

"All of the great leaders have had one characteristic in common: it was the willingness to confront unequivocally the major anxiety of their people in their time. This, and not much else, is the essence of leadership." – John Kenneth Galbraith

In 1956 the Chicago Tribune began to publish an advice column titled *Dear Abby*, which continues to this day. Pauline Phillips wrote the initial column under the pen name "Abigail Van Buren." Today her daughter, Jeanne Phillips, carries forward the legacy.

In one letter to Abby, a young man wrote that he was in love with two women, having an affair with both, and wondered how he would ever choose between the two. He wanted advice but added, "Please don't give me any of that morality stuff." To which Abby fired a rocket in reply: "Morality is what distinguishes human beings from animals. Please consult a veterinarian."[75]

If morality is part of what distinguishes human beings from animals, we might equally say that empathy is what makes leadership truly transformational. If we reduce leadership to building systems, setting policies, and developing good business practices, then all we really need is a manual to run the machinery, and the occasional mechanic to fix it. But most leadership involves leading people who have lives beyond the workplace or the mission of the organization. Our co-workers have marriages and children, aging parents, and mental health issues.[76] They get sick, their moods swing, and their efficiency fluctuates. Staff members in businesses, non-profit organizations, and churches alike do not function like computers and photocopiers, though computers and photocopiers can also seem temperamental at times.

If Abby notes that morality is what distinguishes humans from animals, I might also suggest that empathy is what distinguishes leaders from technicians. Transformational leaders listen to those whom they lead, care for them, and adapt (almost daily at times) to the real-life realities of human lives.

> *Leadership involves leading people who have lives beyond the workplace and beyond the mission of the organization.*

Maya Angelou powerfully noted on one occasion: "I've learned that people will forget what you said, people will forget what you did, but people will never forget how you made them feel." Connection with other people, which forms the foundation for any meaningful long-term collaboration, depends far less on contractual expectations (what some would call transactional leadership) and far more on emotional sensitivities. But this compassion is not a switch to flip within ourselves. It emerges from personal authenticity and vulnerability.

In one of the most-watched TED talks in history, Brené Brown concludes that we can't be compassionate unless we're authentic. Being real with people, being authentic and vulnerable is not only essential to connection but also *precedes* compassion. Until we are kind to ourselves first—not as an expression of narcissism but thinking generously of ourselves without shame or judgment—we can rarely be kind or truly empathetic with others.[77] Authenticity precedes empathy. Once again this is not new. We see it in the life of Jesus as well.

One of the beautiful words used several times in Matthew's Gospel to describe the ministry and leadership of Jesus is *compassion*. In Matthew 9:36 we read: "When Jesus saw the crowds, he had *compassion* on them, because they were harassed and helpless, like sheep without a shepherd." A few chapters later, "When Jesus landed [his boat] and saw a large crowd, he had *compassion* on them and healed their sick" (Matthew 14:14). A chapter later, he sees people who had been following him for three days. They had nothing to eat and were evidently hungry. Rather than send them off to fend for themselves, Jesus "had *compassion* for these people" and instructed his disciples to feed them (Matthew 15:32). On yet another occasion, as Jesus was leaving the city of Jericho, two blind men cried out to him for healing and "Jesus had *compassion* on them and touched their eyes. Immediately they received their sight and followed him" (Matthew 20:34).

We don't need occurrences of the word *compassion* to know that Jesus modeled empathy wherever he went. People flocked to him not only because he was a teacher and performed miracles but also because he listened, he cared, and he responded. He connected with the common folk. Jesus was neither aloof nor separated from the people. He did not build his kingdom from a penthouse suite in a high-rise building.

He did not spend all of his time with bankers, brokers, and board members. To the contrary, he built his kingdom on the back of empathy—love, listening, care, compassion, attentiveness, and responsiveness.

In transformational leadership, empathy occurs at two levels. First, it's empathy for those we lead directly; our own teams and those for whom we have direct responsibility. But secondly, it's empathy for end-users of the products or programs we might develop.

David and Tom Kelley teach creativity, and have been instrumental in guiding a remarkably wide range of innovative design projects from Steve Jobs' computer mouse to can openers for the elderly, and super-cheap and portable baby incubators that are saving lives in India and Nepal. But among their core principles is "empathize with your end-user."[78] We come up with greater ideas when we walk a mile in the shoes of those we'd like to serve. That means standing in railway stations watching how travelers pass through turnstiles to see what works (and what doesn't) for them, before designing new equipment. It means meeting with customers and clients to see their needs and hear their suggestions.

Doug Dietz helps lead design and development of high-tech medical imaging systems for GE Healthcare. A few years ago, as his division completed building, delivering, and installing MRI scanners to various hospitals, he decided to watch as patients came for their tests. Only then did he notice the fear that many children had of being pushed into the scary machine. Indeed, as many as 80 percent of pediatric patients had to be sedated.

Moved with empathy, Doug set out to redesign the scanner. Prototype after prototype finally resulted in scanners that looked more like a pirate adventure or a cylindrical spaceship for children than a cold and frightening piece of equipment.[79]

Empathy extends well beyond our team-members. Transformational leaders also seek to offer it to customers, clients, congregants, and kids. Empathy is an attitude that connects us with people and gives us authority in their lives. Simon Sinek writes:

> There is a pattern that exists in the organizations that achieve the greatest success, the ones that outmaneuver and out-innovate their competitors, the ones that command the greatest respect from inside and outside their organizations, the ones with the highest loyalty and lowest churn and the ability to weather nearly every storm or challenge. These exceptional organizations all have cultures in which the leaders provide cover from above and the people on the ground look out for each other. This is the reason they are willing to push hard and take the kinds of risks they do. And the way any organization can achieve this is with *empathy.* [80]

> *Empathy is an attitude that connects us with people and gives us authority in their lives.*

Empathy brings out the best in others. It has a direct impact on team health and the successful completion of the mission of the organization. It is not a nicety but a necessity, and has several key elements that we should consider. Those elements include listening, caring, and responding. It's simple enough to identify, but so much more difficult to implement with consistency.

LISTENING

Steven Sample has suggested that "the average person suffers from three delusions: (1) That he is a good driver, (2) that he has a good sense of humor, and (3) that he is a good listener. Most people however, including many leaders, are terrible listeners."[81]

Listening has become one of the lost arts of leadership. Far too many leaders default to talking rather than listening; to telling rather than hearing. But artful listening plays a powerful role in transformational leadership and lies at the heart of empathy. Henri Nouwen got it exactly right when he said: "Somewhere we know that without silence words lose their meaning, and without listening speaking no longer heals."

There is, of course, potential for misunderstanding. Sympathetic listening by a leader can be misinterpreted by his or her followers as giving assent. Franklin Roosevelt suffered especially from this problem.[82] People often wrongly assumed that they had his personal support, when they did not. But artful listening—an expression of genuine empathy—can prove powerful and transformational.

Empathy, at its core, involves walking a while in the shoes of another. It's more than sympathy, which is literally to "suffer alongside" (to feel *for* someone). Empathy is to "suffer within" like the other person (to feel *with* them). It's to enter their world, and this surely begins with deep listening and real understanding.

In their bestseller *Crucial Conversations*, Kerry Patterson and his colleagues observe that sometimes we get so caught up in the *content* of a crucial conversation that we fail to see the *conditions*. People say harsh things. Sometimes their candor has a hurtful edge to it and we can easily react. Our defensive shields go up. We hear an accusation and we immediately assume certain motives—"They said this because..." Whether it be true or not, we assume the worst. We heard the content and were so quickly captivated by it that we failed to identify the *conditions* that gave rise to the conversation in the first place. Those *conditions* vary greatly from person to person. Perhaps someone is dealing with serious marital conflict, or a scary health issue, or grief and

Transformational leaders create safe places where crucial conversations don't have to become let-downs or show-downs.

loss. Perhaps they have children whom they're deeply worried about, or they're feeling the strain of caring for aging parents. The *conditions* are always part of the conversation, though we may be oblivious to them. So, *content* is what we hear, but the *conditions* provide the real context for hearing.

Patterson adds: "In truth, most of us have trouble dual-processing (simultaneously watching for content and conditions)—especially when both stakes and emotions are high."[83] Often, as conversations become more serious or intense, the response from people is either silence (masking real feelings, avoiding sensitive subjects, or withdrawing from a conversation altogether) or violence (dominating a conversation, labeling other people, or attacking by belittling or threatening them).[84] Either way, silence or violence reflects that people feel unsafe, disempowered, devalued, or misunderstood. Behind it all, hidden beneath the surface in many instances, are conditions or experiences that shape the moment.[85]

Transformational leaders seek to create safe places where crucial conversations don't have to become let-downs or show-downs. And the pathway to safety is empathy expressed first in listening. As we genuinely enter into the world of others, to understand them, we open the way to authentic conversations.

Stephen Covey's Habit #5 has become proverbial in leadership circles: "Seek first to understand, then to be understood." It assumes listening on the part of the leader. Covey suggests that we struggle with this simple principle because most people listen with the intent to reply, not to understand.[86] But empathy listens well.

As World War II raged, Dietrich Bonhoeffer, the famous Lutheran pastor in Germany who was arrested and eventually executed for plotting against Hitler, wrote: "We must learn to regard people less in the light of what they do or omit to do, and more in the light of what they suffer."[87] But to regard people in light of their personal lives and experiences requires us to *know about* their personal lives and experiences. This doesn't happen by talking but by listening.

In 1995, Daniel Goleman published important ground-breaking work in his book *Emotional Intelligence: Why it Can Matter More Than IQ*. For years, many people had assumed falsely that intellectual cleverness was the chief hallmark of leadership; that the smartest individuals made the greatest leaders. Goleman dismantled this perception. He argued powerfully and convincingly that in fact "emotional intelligence"[88] (what he called EQ rather than IQ) is a greater indicator of likely leadership success. Engineers, chemists, and physicists may be some of the most intelligent people on the planet but this does not assure that they will also rise to positions of significant leadership. Indeed, most of them work on teams and in organizations for other people, because leadership depends more heavily on self-awareness and social skills. Our ability to understand ourselves and read people allows us to best lead people.

> *If we are really listening to what people are saying, we need to be students of their facial expressions, gestures, posture, and other non-verbal elements.*

Adam Grant, the renowned and highly-awarded professor in organizational psychology at the Wharton School of the University of Pennsylvania, makes a similar observation. In his book *Originals* he discusses the impressive abilities of child prodigies but notes the following.

> Child prodigies, it turns out, rarely go on to change the world. When psychologists study history's most eminent and influential people, they discover that many of them weren't unusually gifted as children…. Although child prodigies are often rich in both talent and ambition, what holds them back from moving the world forward is that they don't learn to be original. As they perform in Carnegie Hall, win the science Olympics, and become chess champions, something tragic happens: Practice makes perfect, but it doesn't make new.[89]

Child prodigies, it turns out, generally fail to change the world — or offer transformational leadership — because they often lack originality and just as often lack the social skills (because they've been marginalized from their peers) to lead effectively. Transformational leadership requires particular social skills, all of which can be learned. And high on that list of social skills is listening.

We might also note that real listening also involves watching and observing. Empathy involves understanding the latent needs within people, even if they cannot expressly articulate those needs. Often, by watching and observing their actions, we can learn things we'd never discover through a line of questions or even simple conversation.

Dr. Albert Mehrabian, author of *Silent Messages*, conducted several now-famous studies on nonverbal communication. He found that 7 percent of any message is conveyed through the actual words, 38 percent through certain vocal elements, and 55 percent through nonverbal elements (facial expressions, gestures, posture, etc.).[90] If we are really listening to what people are saying, we need to be students of their facial expressions, gestures, tone of voice, posture, and other non-verbal elements.

We call it body-*language* for a reason. When people stand at a distance, turned away from us, with arms crossed across their chest, and struggling to make eye-contact, it's clear that something is going on, even if they say "I'm fine." Of course, parents see this all the time and have to work through it. But in congregations, workplaces, and families we must decide whether we really want to invest the struggle or not. Transformational leaders, committed to producing change and building lives, know that engagement is not an option.

Listening to both words and body-language is but the first step of empathy. It must be followed then by authentic caring. Empathy is not simply about gathering information about other people, but identifying how we might best support them and care for them.

CARING

In the 2017 movie musical *The Greatest Showman*, Hugh Jackman played the part of Phineas Taylor Barnum. The movie recounts (with considerable artistic license) the formation and rise of the popular Barnum & Bailey Circus, but specifically the initial life and vision of P.T. Barnum.

Throughout the story, James Gordon Bennett (the founder, editor, and publisher of the *New York Herald*)

> *Care creates a powerful culture.*

is a consistent critic of the circus. He has little admiration for Barnum, believing that the showman is simply exploiting unusual people for his own financial gain. But with time, the crusty Bennett comes to appreciate that Barnum actually cares for these people who have been hidden and marginalized by society. Initially, Bennett derisively describes Barnum's "freak show" as a circus but, in a touching moment that becomes a defining moment in the story, he comes to see Barnum and the circus as "a celebration of humanity."

Transformational leaders care for those in their charge, with genuine empathy and compassion. They listen because they care, and they care because they know that no mission of the organization is greater than the responsibility the leader of the organization has for those who work within the organization.

All my Christian life I've heard people repeat: "*The Church is the only organization in the world that exists for the sake of its non-members.*"[91] But is this true? The logic is self-defeating. By this thinking, the Church exists for unbelievers until they become believers, at which time they suddenly no longer matter because all the attention diverts to other unbelievers. The superficially noble sentiment of existing for the sake of non-members is starkly at odds with the New Testament image of a community whose greatest testimony to the Gospel is the way that they love each other (John 13:35).

In a similar way, if transformational leaders care only for the client or the customer (and even then, only until the sale is made), then their teams will inevitably suffer from low morale and productivity. Furthermore, their staff will probably turn-over, and clients are unlikely to return.

Care creates a powerful culture. When people feel cared for, they feel compelled. As Dr. Cornel West, the American philosopher, political activist, social critic, author, and public intellectual says, "You can't lead the people if you don't love the people. You can't save the people if you don't serve the people."

Years ago, my wife (Kim) was diagnosed with cancer. We had just moved across Australia from Perth to Sydney, where I would begin my career and calling as a New Testament professor. We'd been in the city for just a few weeks, and knew nobody. In the chaos of the crisis we reached out to the young pastor of a small church we had visited the Sunday before. He and his wife watched our two young boys while we went to receive the grim news from a specialist. Then the church rallied behind us. For the next three or four months people—many of them complete strangers to us—brought meals every night to our home.

That compassion and care overwhelmed us. After Kim's quick surgery, not so quick radiotherapy, and extended chemotherapy, we joked about which churches we'd like to visit and "try out." We'd been loved straight into the church at Epping. Their profound care completely compelled us.

Have you ever said to yourself, "The people around here care too much about me. I'm leaving!"? None of us are quick to leave when people genuinely care. But when we feel undervalued, unappreciated, unknown, or isolated, we're much more inclined to seek more supportive communities elsewhere.

> *None of us are quick to leave when people genuinely care.*

This takes us back to the adage that people join an organization but leave a manager. When the leader fails in his or her responsibility of care, they not only fail the individual but also the organization.

How do transformational leaders care?

We might care in a range of ways, not all of which come naturally to us. Many male leaders bring a fix-it mentality to their leadership. Ask husbands who have wandered into these deep waters when their wives have just wanted them to listen. A natural caring impulse for many people is to jump in and resolve a problem that someone has. If there's conflict, we give advice or might even get involved. Fix it. If there's financial strain, we might open our own wallet or set up a GoFundMe campaign online. Fix it. But care is more than problem-solving. Care is first of all about connection.

Brené Brown, the renowned social researcher from the University of Houston cited earlier in this chapter, has concluded that connection lies at the very heart of our humanity. Strong connection with other people produces courage and creativity within us. It makes us secure and enables us to be authentic and vulnerable. This, in turn, allows us to manage shame and fear in positive ways. Conversely, lack of connection exacerbates our isolation, drives us within ourselves, accentuates shame, and magnifies fear. People who know that they are accepted and loved, handle their inner brokenness (which we all have) much more deliberately and effectively.[92]

When we express empathy by caring for others, we build connection; this building block of human experience. We don't treat people like pieces of machinery, assuming that they will function at high capacity all of the time irrespective of health issues, family issues, or emotional challenges they might face. The people around us are first of all human *beings*, not human *doings*. Their value and significance is not derived from their productivity or output in the workplace. Their work, in most instances, is how they make a living, not how they make a life. Transformational leaders understand this, and even encourage it. Surely no workplace has higher value than a marriage or a family. Marriages and families (not businesses or congregations) are the core units of society. When we sacrifice their health and well-being, we jeopardize everything we work for and depend on.

Businesses need to make profits, and these profits are often described as "the bottom line."[93] But profits are not the reason that businesses exist. Money has no intrinsic value. It serves only as a mechanism for something greater; the enhancement of the lives of those who own or work in the company. When we begin to think that "making money" is our business, we have lost sight of the entire purpose of our economic system. Money is ultimately a mere tool with which we care for others. Our products and services ought to care for customers and clients. In turn, their money ought to provide care for the workers. This is a fundamental application of the "care" principle.

We see an extreme violation of this simple principle in the sweatshops of southeast Asia.

Sweatshop slavery has been around since the industrial age of the early 19th century. Even today, many people are either tricked or trafficked into sweatshop labor.

In July 2008, an undercover operation by Australian Channel 7 News exposed the horrifying conditions for 1,200 workers at the Nike Hytex factory in Malaysia. Reporters found that the workers were not Malaysian, but mostly from Thailand, Cambodia, and Vietnam. These laborers had all been lied to by recruiters who promised high wages, a good life, and freedom to leave when they wanted. None of that was true. The workers were forced to sign contracts they could not understand, were paid poorly, and had no ability to leave until they repaid their travel expenses and various "fees" which they could not repay on their minimal wages. It produced a cycle of inescapable slavery and poverty, with only the management of the factory (and the Nike company) making money. Meanwhile, the workers toiled in terrible conditions, lived in cramped rat-infested quarters (up to twenty-six people crammed into a room smaller than a classroom), and had unsanitary showers and hole-in-the-wall bathrooms. At times, the factory would withhold the workers' pay for months.

Nike denied any knowledge of these inhumane conditions, conducted its own investigation, and quickly moved workers to approved housing, returned passports, paid wages, and offered flights back home for the workers — but only after the embarrassing story broke.[94]

It may seem an extreme example, but perhaps it makes the point. How easily and subtly we can lose focus and cease to care for those whom we lead. Without much thought (and that's the problem) we can begin to consider people no more highly than the automated systems that churn out our products.

> Leaders who genuinely care stand out like beacons of virtue and hope in an otherwise dark world.

In such an environment, transformational leaders who genuinely care stand out like beacons of virtue and hope in an otherwise fairly dark world.

This theme of "care" goes back a long way in Scripture, too. In ancient Israel, landowners were specifically instructed not to harvest the corners of their fields. We read in Leviticus 23:22, "When you reap the harvest of your land, do not reap to the very edges of your field or gather the gleanings of your harvest. Leave them for the poor and for the foreigner residing among you. I am the LORD your God." This prescription certainly helped the poor in the community. It provided them at least some marginal way to feed themselves. But it surely also served (in practice) as a small benefit for those who worked the land. It recognized the importance of the welfare of the workers.

Similarly, in an economy driven by day-laborers whose daily work often provided only enough to buy daily food for themselves and their families, landowners were expressly prohibited from withholding payment. Deuteronomy 24:15 stipulated: "Pay them their wages each day before sunset, because they are poor and are counting on it. Otherwise they may cry to the LORD against you, and you will be guilty of sin."

Transformational leaders both understand and practice empathy; listening, caring, and also responding.

RESPONDING

Non-responsive empathy is not empathy at all. When we truly hear what others say, it inevitably and irresistibly drives us to some kind of action. Parents experience this every day. When our children fall and injure themselves, most of us spring into action. We respond. We feel their pain (and perhaps fear the worst), and it motivates us.

In the New Testament, James writes: "If a brother or sister is without clothing and in need of daily food, and one of you says, 'Go in peace, be warm and be filled,' and yet you do not give them what is necessary for their body, what use is that?" (James 2:15-16, NASB). The ancient text identified a common human problem — indifference. Apathy and empathy are complete opposites. Real empathy steps up and steps in. It engages. It responds. Having listened and cared, it takes action.

On February 23, 2018, shortly after Nikolas Cruz had killed 17 people at Marjory Stoneman Douglas High School in Parkland, Florida, Bryan Logan wrote an article for *Business Insider* about President Donald Trump's engagement with victims of the February 14 (Valentine's Day and Ash Wednesday) shooting. The article contrasted Samantha Fuentes (a victim of the shooting, recovering from her wounds in hospital) and Andrew Pollack (a father whose daughter died in the shooting). The president called Fuentes on the phone and it didn't go well. She described the call with these words: "Talking to the President, I've never been so unimpressed by a person in my life. He didn't make me feel better in the slightest." On the other hand Andrew Pollack, who attended a special gathering in the West Wing at the White House told reporters that President Trump, "showed us nothing but love." [95]

In writing his story, Logan noted that, "The conversation around what some have described as Trump's *empathy deficit* resurfaced when photographers captured images of personal notes Trump held during the White House listening session with students and family members." [96] The notecard listed five talking points for the president, the last being "I hear you." Critics claimed that the president needed a notecard reminder to show compassion.

Politics aside, the perceived level of empathy experienced by Fuentes and Pollack, deeply affected their respect for the president and his leadership. Empathy is not incidental or secondary.

Transformational leaders, as we've noted before, do not see people as means to an end (machines with flesh and blood) but as partners in a process towards change and changed lives. They listen, care, and then respond appropriately.

One of the great stories in Scripture is the Exodus story — the story of Israel being delivered from slavery in Egypt. The narrative spans twelve chapters in the Bible (Exodus 1-12) but one of the early pivot points is Exodus 2:24-25. The Israelites had suffered greatly under bondage, and they cried out to God and then we read: "So God *heard* their groaning; and God *remembered* His covenant with Abraham, Isaac, and Jacob. And God *saw* the sons of Israel, and God *took notice* of them" (NASB). The following ten chapters chronicle the response and action of God to set his people free. The passage oozes empathy; God listening, remembering, seeing, taking notice…and then taking action.

What actions might empathy produce? In the workplace, it might involve flexible hours, family leave, cost-of-living salary increases, better pacing of projects, and a myriad of other responses.

Ed Catmull described the culture at Pixar when they were working on the film *Toy Story 2*. It was a frenetic season. In his own words:

> For six months, our employees rarely saw their families. We worked deep into the night, seven days a week. Despite two hit movies, we were conscious of the need to prove ourselves, and everyone gave everything they had. With several months to go, the staff was exhausted and starting to fray.
>
> One morning in June, an overtired artist drove to work with his infant child strapped into the back seat, intending to deliver the baby to day care on the way.

Sometime later, after he had been at work for a few hours, his wife (also a Pixar employee) happened to ask him how the drop-off had gone—which is when he realized that he'd left their child in the car in the broiling Pixar parking lot. They rushed out to find the baby unconscious and poured cold water over him immediately. Thankfully, the child was okay, but the trauma of this moment—the what-could-have-been—was imprinted deeply on my brain. Asking this much of our people, even when they wanted to give it, was not acceptable. I had expected the road to be rough, but I had to admit that we were coming apart. By the time the film was complete, a full third of the staff would have some kind of repetitive stress injury.[97]

Pixar made significant cultural changes after this episode. Listening (seeing), caring, and responding were crucial to the ongoing vitality of the organization. They had pushed their people—driven by a common vision and looming deadlines—beyond good or reasonable limits. So they renewed their commitment to the health and well-being of the team and instituted strategic changes. They heard, they cared, and they responded.

FAILED EMPATHY

It would be remiss not to briefly address what we might called "failed empathy." This refers not to one's failure to empathize but rather to the way that misapplied empathy might undermine both the leader and the organization.

Empathy does not require acquiescence to those who would subvert the mission of the organization. Sometimes a team member is so wounded, or so afraid, or has such a long history of non-productivity, that they lose their way within the organization. They hang on to their job, but they function like a slow-leaking poison among their peers or colleagues. This can happen in workplaces, church-places, and families, too.

Empathy is not the unwillingness (as a transformational leader) to release someone—even to ask a child to leave the home—but to understand them and hear them and work with them before reaching that decision too quickly. But there comes a time when action and response is required.

In 2016, I met the parents of a young 20-year-old man whose drug habits were destroying the home life. He stole from them, was belligerent and abusive towards them, and sometimes exhibited violence. They felt terrified and distraught in their own home. They could see no way forward. They had supported their son and gotten counseling for him, to no avail. A group of us assured these parents that they had indeed gone above

> *Empathy does not require acquiescence to those who would subvert the mission of the organization.*

and beyond the call of duty, and advised them that if they really loved both their son and the family, they would need to cut him loose and put him on the streets. But they couldn't imagine doing that. "He'll never survive," they said. Of course, they were primarily echoing what their son had told them. They had a family contract with him that included sending him from the home if he lost his sobriety, but misguided and false empathy restrained them from taking that step. And the nightmare continued for both them and their son.

This certainly happens in leadership in every sphere of life and society. The tender heart can immobilize us. It may restrain us from taking action that is absolutely best for the organization as a whole.

R. Judson Carlberg, president of Gordon College noted that "when justified by a good and fair performance-evaluation system, appropriate terminations accelerate trust within a community."[98] Others are always watching because others are always affected. A failure to take action can be as undermining to morale as premature or thoughtless action. We look to leaders not only to set the vision but also to manage the efforts and relationships on the team, bearing in mind that all of us have different strengths and capacities.

Empathy is core to transformational leadership. For some people it smacks of mushiness and unproductive sentimentality, but truly transformational leaders give it priority and understand how essential it is to producing change and building lives. Empathy, preceded by authenticity, is not a luxury. Nor is it the product of personality. All leaders can learn it, develop it, practice it, implement it, and be better for it. And all organizations achieve their mission more successfully because of it.

CHAPTER SUMMARY

Transformational leaders have a fundamental commitment to building lives. This expresses itself in empathetic leadership, which listens, cares, and responds. Listening is not just catching what people say and reading between the lines, but also reading body language and watching moods and actions. Caring leaders develop genuine compassion for their team members, customers, clients, and families. They recognize the complexities that we all face in life, and know that sales or services come and go but lives have an inherently greater importance. Transformational leaders also know that responding involves more than quickly acquiescing to any request or need that we hear. It requires consideration of the real issues in the lives of others and engaging appropriately.

SOME POSSIBLE EXERCISES

Listening

If you'd like to strengthen your listening skills, be fully present for someone in a difficult conversation. Don't try to fix anything. Don't dominate the conversation. Listen more than speak. Afterwards, make some notes for yourself about their eye contact, body language, posture, tone, and words. What did you miss in the moment? What might you do better in the next crucial conversation? Repeat this practice once a week for a while.

Caring

Brainstorm with one or two other people ways that you could create a more caring environment in your home, church, or workplace. Make a list of at least a dozen ideas, then choose one or two and decide how to implement them in the next week. Remember, action deferred often becomes action denied.

Responding

Empathy and compassion don't come easily for everyone. Extend yourself in a specific act of compassion *at least twice in the week ahead.* Look for the needs. Take a specific action — perhaps a handwritten note, a small gift, or some time over coffee to listen. Put it on your calendar (if necessary) to repeat this exercise in the first week of each month for the next six months.

NOTES

Key thoughts you had while reading this chapter. **Questions** that came up. **Ideas** for personal next steps. **Insights** to discuss with a friend.

_____

_____

_____

_____

_____

Chapter 7

Innovation

"If you're not failing every now and again, it's a sign you're not doing anything very innovative." – Woody Allen

Innovation: *the introduction of something new; a new idea, method, or device.*

If transformational leadership involves "producing change" then it follows that it also requires innovation of the best kind. Creativity and innovation are not the same. Creativity is the ability to think differently and outside the box. Innovation is the ability to make something real and tangible out of creativity. But innovation often gets holstered. Have you found a resistance to innovation, perhaps within yourself or within others? Why do universities, churches, and companies tend to apply the brakes at this point?

Innovation is costly. Companies spend vast amounts of money on research and development, and the dollars and human hours add up quickly. This in itself can make some leaders wary of innovation; high risk without guaranteed return.

On the other hand, some leaders (perhaps many) have fear of failure deeply rooted within them. It's not a matter of financial cost or effort expended. It's all about perception and image. Will people lose respect for a leader who fails? Will such leaders even respect themselves? This internal tug-of-war can also stifle creativity.

Innovation can also be difficult to unleash because our K-12 educational system is unintentionally designed to quench the creative spirit of students and produce conformity.[99] Thus, when we call for people to be creative, they have lost both the confidence and the skills to bring their creativity to the surface.

Between institutional conservatism, personal leadership paranoia, and the stifled spirits of team members, innovation is frequently elusive. But it's the job of the transformational leader to encourage, uncover, nurture, and release creativity and innovation. It's the job of the transformational leader to nurture and unleash thinking.

French philosopher René Descartes (1596-1650) famously wrote *cogito ergo sum*, "I think therefore I am." Philosophers ever since have pondered the truth of this existential declaration.

The Latin term *cogito* ("I think") derives from a combination of two other Latin words *con + agitare*. *Agitare* means to put something in motion, to drive, to impel, to hunt, to chase, to pursue, to toss about, to agitate, to disturb, to rouse, to excite, etc. You get the point. It's a powerful and dynamic word. It assumes a high level of activity and engagement. It moves people. Good thinking (*cogito*), real thinking (*cogito*), always does.

The transformational leader need not be the most creative member of the team, but they *will* find ways to draw to the surface the creativity and best thinking of others. As always, this is equally as true of raising children as leading a team of work colleagues.

How do we unearth and liberate the latent creativity within us all? At least four factors come into play that require increasing security and maturity on the part of the leader.

ENCOURAGE OWNERSHIP

I love the story of Richard Montanez. He came to the United States as a young Mexican immigrant but dropped out of

> *The transformational leader encourages, uncovers, nurtures, and releases creativity and innovation.*

High School because he didn't speak English well enough to understand his teachers. Instead, he took a job in 1976 as a janitor at the Frito-Lay Rancho Cucamonga plant in California.

Montanez grew up near Ontario, California picking grapes to help support his family and eating at a communal table with six or seven other families each day. In an interview with Fox News he said: "My dream was to drive the trash truck." But one day, while cleaning at the Frito-Lay factory he heard a video message from the president telling employees to "act like an owner." It struck a chord with him.

In a serendipitous moment, one of the assembly line machines broke, leaving some Cheetos without their bright orange cheese dust. Richard took some of the unfinished Cheetos home with him and had the idea to coat them with chili powder. His friends loved the hot Cheetos and urged him to share the idea.

The president agreed to give Richard a shot at pitching his new product idea, and gave him two weeks to prepare a presentation for the company executives. Richard and his wife made a trip to the public library and borrowed a book on business strategies. They pored over it and gave themselves a crash course in marketing.

When the day of the presentation arrived, Montanez put on his $3 tie (the first he had ever owned) and went in to sell his hot Cheetos idea to the company executives. The rest is history. His Flamin' Hot Cheetos became Frito-Lay's top-selling product.

Today Montanez is an executive of the company he once worked for as a janitor and spearheads the Frito-Lay Hispanic marketing team.[100]

The story is powerful for several reasons. Montanez took a risk as a lowly janitor to set up a meeting with the president. But the president also took a risk to let Montanez make the presentation, and then to follow through on making the new product line. However, the innovation at Frito-Lay started with an invitation to employees to "act like an owner."

Ownership, in this case, means more than having a financial interest in the organization. It's a mindset. It's love for the purpose and mission of the organization. It's full engagement in the organization. It's wanting the best for the organization and therefore taking responsibility for it. It's pouring our creativity and innovation into the organization.

Workers and team members will only engage to this level when their leaders encourage and allow for it.

Very few leaders would argue against this position. In theory, we all know that this would be enormously energizing and exciting for an organization. If team members felt free to "act like an owner" and felt liberated from bureaucratic red-tape, they could soar like eagles. We all know that this has wonderful potential, and few people would oppose it in theory. However, reality has a way of messing with theoretical commitments. Politics and self-interest have a way of applying brakes to real creativity. And the very leaders who say publicly "Act like an owner" oftentimes privately stifle it.

Transformational leadership is not oblivious to workplace politics, but it confronts it and systematically seeks to dismantle it.

When our brightest and best team members take ownership we unleash a creative genie from the bottle. When they are told to "stay within their lanes" and "stick to their job description" we surrender true innovation.

This challenges the controlling leader. Ironically, the more that we seek to control or micromanage an environment, the less healthy that environment becomes. For example, in raising children we discover that parental control must be on a sliding scale as our kids get older. Parents who micromanage their kids' time and space eventually stunt the healthy development of their children. The same is true in organizations. Dan Allender correctly notes that "a controlling leader always gets what he deserves—the bare minimum and conformity without creativity."[101]

We have all sorts of unhealthy reasons to become controlling as leaders. Sometimes, it's a way to grasp and exercise power. At a subconscious level (perhaps) it's a case of "I'll show 'em who's boss!" Other times, it may be an irresistible perfectionism that cannot settle for anything sub-standard. Oftentimes, it is fear. Many a leader uses intimidation and manipulation to silence potential critics and to protect their own fiefdom, deeply afraid that someone might actually approach the curtain and discover that the mighty Wizard of Oz is nothing more than a small figure with a loud voice.

The more we control, the less creativity we release. If we are serious about encouraging ownership—building buy-in—we must grapple with the urge to control, and find ways to "expand ownership." This inevitably means that we will employ a range of measures in the workplace that might include creating a flatter communication structure, incentivizing employees for creativity, or building sufficient space and opportunity into the workflow for team members to think creatively.

> *The more we control other people, the less creativity we release.*

Flatter communication structures mean that everyone within an organization (non-profits, churches, and businesses alike) can speak to people across the organization without having to funnel up through multiple levels of bureaucracy. The military have learned the necessity of this on the battlefield. Battlefield officers are authorized to make strategic decisions—sometimes innovative ones—based on the conditions on the ground. When suggestions or requests get delayed or lost in a complex communication chain, lives can be at stake.

Incentivization for creativity also encourages the ownership mentality. Creativity—particularly the innovation that advances our cause—deserves recognition and reward, and nothing takes the wind out of the sails of innovation faster than stolen ideas or suppressed energy.

Incentivization comes in many different forms (money, authority, promotion, additional opportunities, etc.) and the transformational leader will customize the incentive to the personality and preferences of each person. How it looks will be different from person to person, but in every case, it matters.

Finally, space and opportunity for creativity also make a difference. In a 2004 letter announcing the launch of Google, founders Larry Page and Sergey Brin wrote: "We encourage our employees, in addition to their regular projects, to spend 20 percent of their time working on what they think will most benefit Google... This empowers them to be more creative and innovative." Google staff were also given access to an "innovation lab."[102] Few of us have the resources to mimic this practice, but the undergirding philosophy merits careful consideration. If creativity and innovation in this Age of Innovation really matter, then it cannot be relegated to those rare moments of down-time. If we get serious about encouraging a mentality of ownership, then space and opportunity for creative experimentation and innovative reflection will be paramount.

The first step towards building a culture of innovation is to encourage the mindset of ownership; to build within people a commitment to the mission and a pride in the organization, church, or family. The second step is to then take risks.

TAKE RISKS

Some people are serial entrepreneurs. Ideas simply pour out. Creativity comes easily. They've been successful and affirmed enough times that they have the security to try new things. It's relatively easy for them to go where they've never gone before; to take risks.

Others find risk-taking easy because they're narcissists; so self-absorbed and self-confident that it never occurs to them that others might be hesitant or reluctant. We've all seen extreme versions of this personality; the person who is never wrong, never needs to apologize, and never fails (in their own mind). For the extreme narcissist, risk-taking is real but it's never personal. Failure is a speed-bump, and always gets pinned on someone else. That's not transformational leadership.

Innovation always has some risk associated with it. So we must ask ourselves, "How risk-averse are we?"

Risk-management lies at the heart of transformational leadership,

> Risk-management is
> not risk-elimination.

but risk-management does not mean risk-elimination. Risk-elimination is, after all, an impossibility. Every day we face risk. In families, we take a risk (multiple risks) every day that we wake up and send our kids out into the world; health risks, emotional risks, moral risks, and spiritual risks to name but a few. Crossing the road can have an element of risk. Disease lurks in bathrooms and kitchens. People we meet may unknowingly pass along a virus or two. New "friends" will influence the core values of our children. If we give our children or teens access to the web via iPhones or Androids, the risks escalate enormously. Of course, sheltering our children at home doesn't lessen the risks; it simply creates a new set of risks — socialization issues, the capacity to handle a hostile world, limited exposure to growth-inducing experiences. There's no such thing as a risk-free environment. Every day, at every turn, our families make choices and decisions that have risk associated with them.

Businesses deal with the same issues. Any choice to limit innovation carries as much risk as a choice to encourage it. Financial decisions about new hires, marketing strategies and budgets, or expansion to new facilities all carry risk *whatever decisions are made*. Some leaders believe in risk-minimization, since risk-elimination is unrealistic. But risk-minimization is sometimes code for "we'll only do what we've always done." And this pathway, resistant to innovation, sometimes proves costly, if not fatal.

Founded in 1888, the Eastman Kodak company led the world in film-processing throughout the 20th century. It was so successful in its chemical photo-development processes that it commanded 90 percent of the market in its heyday. But in 2012, the company filed for bankruptcy protection. It emerged as a much smaller and leaner company in 2013. Once one of the most powerful companies in the world, in January 2018 Eastman Kodak's market capitalization was just $129 million!

What caused this colossal collapse? Multiple factors contributed to the decline, but analysts often note that "by clinging to traditional photography, Kodak demonstrated that it was too protective of its brand and its original profit source."[103]

The company had actually developed the first prototype of a digital camera in 1975, but it continued to believe that its future lay where its past had been; in film-processing. The company resisted expansion to new fields. Yes, it explored and experimented with new possibilities, but ultimately company leadership refused to let the innovation redefine the direction of the company.[104] The company measured the risks inherent in a major change, evaluated its heritage and legacy, and decided to "play it safe." The irony should not be lost on any of us.

Peter Drucker has said: "If you want something new, you have to stop doing something old." Transformational leaders understand that innovation is not just a luxury, but a core element of producing change in the world. Innovation always carries an element of risk, but it guides us to better anticipate and participate in constructive disruption.

When we release the creativity of those with whom we live or work, we position ourselves to truly raise up a corps of transformational leaders who can lead families, communities, businesses, movements, and nations in significant ways. This requires that we encourage ownership and take risks. But it also assumes that we will allow for failure.

ALLOW FOR FAILURE

We will never unleash creativity in either ourselves or others until we come to terms with failure, and allow for it. Indeed, the most innovative teams assume it. They expect it. They'd be shocked not to have it.

Ty Cobb (1886-1961) leads the all-time career batting average in baseball with .366. George Herman "Babe" Ruth (1895-1948) comes in at #10 with .342. Indeed, only 30 players in all of baseball have finished their careers with an average above .330. What does that mean? Simply that the very best hitters in all of baseball got a base hit about one in every three times they batted. They "failed" two-thirds of the time that they went to the plate.

Michael Jordan, one of the greatest basketball players to ever lace up a pair of shoes, noted "I've missed more than 9000 shots in my career. I've lost almost 300 games. 26 times I've been trusted to take the game winning shot and missed. I've failed over and over and over again in my life. And that is why I succeed."[105]

If we want to encourage innovation and release creativity in our homes, churches, or workplaces, we must allow for failure and see it more as the pathway to success rather than the end of an effort. This will stretch some of us, since one of the greatest fears that some people carry is the fear of failure.

> *See failure as the pathway to success rather than the end of an effort.*

Firstborns in particular (though not exclusively) learn early in life that they get a lot of affirmation for success. People like winners and warm to them, and over time we might start to believe that failure will mean rejection and loss of face. This results in our reluctance to try anything that might fail, or even propose anything that might not succeed. It produces a paralysis, even in a brainstorming environment. "What if they think my idea is stupid? What if my idea clearly won't work? What if my idea is not the best one on the table?" These "what ifs" can defeat us.

Many of us have little tolerance for failure. In some instances, it's because we have no financial margin for trial and error. Perhaps our cash flow as an organization is so tight that everything "has to work." But more often than not, it's a matter of leadership and personality. We just don't have any personal tolerance or taste for failure.

Perhaps it would be helpful to re-frame the process of innovation, not in terms of success or failure but in terms of participation and prototypes. If we realize (and communicate) that any great innovation is the product of multiple iterations and extensive collaboration, then each new thought or suggestion is not an end in itself but a small part of a process.

Consider someone learning to play the guitar. Nobody would tell a guitar novice to think hard about playing and get it perfect before they ever strum, or they won't get another chance. Not at all. The very process of practicing the guitar will involve many missteps and wrong fingering. Nobody expects that a novice will immediately be a virtuoso. But diligence and persistence irons out the errors and develops competence and (sometimes) a master.[106]

Tom and David Kelley, two brothers whom I've mentioned earlier, launched IDEO, one of the world's leading innovation and design firms, as well as the *d.school* at Stanford University. They've taught innovation and creativity for a long time and discovered the reluctance of people to pursue any idea that might fail. Many of us resist the label "creative" because our self-worth and self-image are tied closely to success.

Failure is not fun. Nobody enjoys it. However, professors in Stanford's *d.school* periodically remind students that "Failure sucks, but instructs."[107] Interestingly, in Silicon Valley and other places where venture capitalists gather, "failure conferences" are cropping up. There is growing recognition that if we analyze failure well, there's a trove of information to glean, and powerful lessons to be learned. In the same way that Thomas Edison went through a thousand iterations of the incandescent light-bulb before he perfected it, so failure can prove incredibly powerful on the road to meaningful innovation.

Perfectionists find failure virtually intolerable. They assume that if team members do their homework and think hard enough about all the possibilities, they cannot fail. Or perhaps it's a matter of effort. If only everyone would work harder, then every idea would succeed. Of course, reasonable people know how unreasonable this is. But when we build a culture of such high expectations, we shut down risk-taking and innovation.

For decades I believed that perfectionism was a virtue. Not until well into my 40s did I begin to suspect that it might actually be a vice. It isolates us from each other. It demotivates us. And it burns us out.[108]

> *Failure must become our teacher, not our executioner.*

Some time ago I was reading *Popular Woodworking* magazine. That particular issue included a delightful article by Nancy Hiller in which she reflected on a century-old piece of simple furniture that she owned. The chest of drawers, pre-dating 1885 and made of deal (a nondescript term for very common softwoods) had some delightful handmade sliding dovetails and stub tenons; clever joints holding it all together. But some of the joints were less carefully constructed than others. Then Hiller wrote this:

> These dovetails, which were clearly made by an accomplished craftsman intent on getting the job done,

remind me that in the universe of making things, utility is no less worthy a goal than fine craft. Amidst the relentless drive to do better, it's easy to lose sight of the grace that characterizes our very ability to make things, however imperfectly, not to mention the blessings offered by even the most basic material artifacts. Yes, the things we make reflect who we are, at least to a degree—and who wants to be defined by radical imperfection? But there's a conceit in being so wrapped up in the tightness and proportions of a joint that we lose sight of the bigger picture, which includes those who will use the things we make.[109]

Transformational leaders promote innovation (in part) by making room for failure, failing forward, and accepting radical imperfection.[110] They see failure as opportunity. It becomes our teacher, not our executioner. In one sense, as Kevin Cashman notes, "Failure does not exist. It is life attempting to teach us some new lessons or trying to point some new directions."[111]

Venture capitalists understand this. They are people and firms willing to put money into start-up businesses that banks would consider too risky. Perhaps the best-known venture capitalists are the panel members on the television show *Shark Tank* where contestants pitch their creative new ideas and seek investment dollars from the four panelists. In the much larger world of venture capitalism, venture capital firms in 2014 invested $47 billion (yes, *billion*) into new start-ups, knowing that two-thirds of those start-ups would fold.[112] Yet, they do it to encourage innovation and, hopefully, make a huge profit on the few creative ideas that take off (e.g. Facebook, Twitter, PayPal, Pinterest, Uber).

How much, as a transformational leader, do you allow for failure?

Jesus, the son of God, certainly allowed for it more than many of us do. In the course of his ministry, he watched his disciples fail repeatedly. They failed in faith. They failed in friendship. They failed in things they tried. They failed in leadership. They failed in understanding. Three years of night and day contact with Jesus, and his followers still didn't seem ready to graduate. Yet, he kept them, and kept working with them, and trusted them to ultimately carry the Gospel forward, which they did.

However, while ideas, efforts, deadlines, and expectations could all fail, transformational leadership does not have the same latitude with ethical failure. Innovation must never be at the expense of a true moral and ethical compass.

> *Innovation is not simply a matter of achieving more, but doing so in the most moral and ethical manner possible.*

INNOVATION AND ETHICS

The fourth "I" of historical transformational leadership is "Intellectual Stimulation." In addition to innovation, it includes constantly challenging followers to higher levels of moral and ethical performance. It's not simply a matter of achieving more or doing more, but achieving more in the most moral and ethical manner possible. This moral element is crucial for transformational leadership. It's what keeps the whole ship from listing dangerously to one side. In the pursuit of innovation, it can be easy to compromise core ethical principles.

We see this with regularity in various fields of research. For example, medical innovation has experimented with new applications of stem-cell research and its possible curative properties. But while science has charged ahead, the moral and ethical questions of this new technology have lagged far behind. Just because we *can* do something, doesn't mean that we *should* do something.

Similarly, *planned obsolescence* in industrial design and economics is a policy of planning or designing a product with an artificially limited useful life, so it will become obsolete (that is, unfashionable or no longer functional) after a certain period of time. This requires consumers to replace the product at regular intervals. It's innovative. If the washing machine manufacturer replaces steel bearings with plastic parts, then the washing machine will only last three or four years. The shorter the life-span, the more units consumers will have to buy. Of course, it's cheaper to manufacture plastic bearings and plastic drums than steel ones, but the end result is that the poorest consumers (who can only afford the flimsiest products) will actually end up paying the most for their clean clothes over a lifetime.

Innovation must always grapple deeply with ethics, and transformational leaders take this charge seriously.

THE SUPPRESSION OF INNOVATION

Some people believe that the American education system is fundamentally broken. Authors Tony Wagner and Ted Dintersmith, in their book *Most Likely to Succeed*, provide a compelling portrait of the American educational landscape, and it's not pretty. They argue, rather convincingly, that our educational system was designed in 1893 "to educate large numbers of immigrants and refugees from farms for basic citizenship and for jobs in a growing industrial economy."[113] The system has not undergone any fundamental change in the past 130 years, despite the major shifts to an *information* economy and now an *innovation* economy.

In short, Wagner and Dintersmith claim that we're still teaching students how to meet standardized expectations (factory-line stuff) and how to perform rote (and repetitive) tasks. And in the midst of this, we have successfully stifled creativity and quenched innovation.

The great irony, of course, is that Wagner and Dintersmith's blunt analysis calls for great creativity and innovation (which has been squashed) to change the monolithic K-12 and

> *The suppression of innovation can only lead us backwards.*

higher education juggernaut. The system is inherently designed to stay stuck.

Many of us in leadership do the same thing. We design systems that favor stability, predictability, and consistency. We create workplace policies and practices (and even family environments) that help us maintain control. We build systems for homeostasis — balance, equilibrium, stability, and "steady as she goes." The cost? The incalculable loss of creativity and innovation.

Our aversion to risk, whether in churches or businesses, makes us resistant to new initiatives and untried pathways. When failure is not permissible, innovation is rarely possible. When we over-commit ourselves financially our risk tolerance diminishes dramatically. In the home, creativity may require both mess and flexibility; more than tired parents can sometimes bear.

The outcome?

The suppression of innovation can only lead us backwards. It makes us fit only for rote tasks. It stymies real growth and progress. It makes us managers, not leaders; responders, not initiators.

One of the well-researched and well-established pillars of transformational leadership is "intellectual stimulation" (creativity and innovation). Scholars and practitioners alike have known for forty years that creativity and innovation lie close to the heart of the strongest leadership. "Business as usual" was a great motto for the industrial age, but it will not suffice in the innovation age.

How are you encouraging and releasing creativity and innovation in your children, workplace, church, or favorite organization?

COMMUNICATION STRUCTURES

Ed Catmull co-founded Pixar Animation Studios and went on to become president of Pixar Animation and Disney Animation when Disney bought Pixar in 2006 for $7.4 billion. Catmull understands the complexity of releasing creativity, but also has a tremendous track record in doing so.

In his book *Creativity, Inc.*, Catmull described his journey from Lucas Films to Pixar and then to Disney/Pixar and the challenges he faced at multiple points to release the innovation of his teams. Among the discoveries he made was this: Don't confuse organizational structures with communication structures.[114] When people use organizational structures to block communication, creativity suffers.

This happens a lot as organizations grow in size. As organizational structures in-crease in complexity, people at the top of the chart have less and less contact with people further down the line and the lowest tier of workers simply have no access to middle or upper management. Sometimes this is pragmatic in origin, a way to guard the time of executive leaders. Oftentimes it is far more political. It's about "creating lanes" for people to work within; a mechanism for controlling information and minimizing work-arounds. This works against innovation in most instances.

Organizational structures serve a key purpose; delineation of authority lines — who decides what? But communication is foundational to innovation and buy-in throughout an organization. It's one thing to go over the top of a supervisor to get another person to approve an idea or a project. It's something quite different to throw a creative idea into the mix for senior leadership to consider.

> *When people confuse organizational structures with communication structures, creativity suffers.*

As Japan began to rebuild after World War II, an American named W. Edwards Deming coached Japanese industry leaders on quality control. Previously, they had insisted that the assembly-lines should never stop. Lost time meant lost money. Quality control inspectors would try and catch defects before they were shipped, and the results were mediocre at best. Deming turned this on its head.

Deming taught Japanese management that every worker, from assembly-line personnel to the president, shared responsibility for quality control. If anyone spotted a problem, they should be expected (and empowered) to stop the assembly-line and fix the problem. To make this possible, a radical adjustment was made to the assembly-lines. Pull-cords were added that enabled workers on the floor to actually stop the production to address a problem before multiple mistakes were made. Instead of merely watching faulty or inferior products pass down the line, workers could suggest changes, call out problems, and feel the pride of helping to fix what was broken. A simple tenet guided these companies: You don't have to ask permission to take responsibility. This would eventually transform Japanese manufacturing and elevate their products (think Toyota, Lexus, Sony, Canon, Honda, Acura, Casio, Citizen, Nintendo, etc.) to the peak of product development.

Transformational leaders embrace a commitment to innovation, but must grapple with the real possibility that power-based (and politically protected) organizational structures might stifle the very creativity and innovation they desire.

Finally, hoarding ideas rather than sharing them, stunts innovation. This conviction underwrites the American electric car manufacturer Tesla, Inc.

Founded in 2003, Tesla produces electric cars and solar panels. On June 12, 2014, Elon Musk, the chairman, CEO and product architect of the Tesla company issued this remarkable public statement:

Yesterday, there was a wall of Tesla patents in the lobby of our Palo Alto headquarters. That is no longer the case. They have been removed, in the spirit of the open source movement, for the advancement of electric vehicle technology.

Tesla Motors was created to accelerate the advent of sustainable transport. If we clear a path to the creation of compelling electric vehicles, but then lay intellectual property landmines behind us to inhibit others, we are acting in a manner contrary to that goal. Tesla will not initiate patent lawsuits against anyone who, in good faith, wants to use our technology.

When I started out with my first company, I thought patents were a good thing and worked hard to obtain them. And maybe they were good long ago, but too often these days they serve merely to stifle progress, entrench the positions of giant corporations and enrich those in the legal profession, rather than the actual inventors.[115]

We've covered a lot of ground in this chapter, perhaps appropriately. In an age of innovation, some might argue that we need innovation to

> *Transformational leaders do not see themselves as the rear-guard but as the vanguard of culture.*

simply keep up. But I'd like to propose a higher and better motivation. "Keeping up" is always a follower mentality. While survival may provide great motivation for innovation, transformational leaders do not see themselves as the rear-guard but as the vanguard of culture. And such leaders view innovation not as a way to preserve what we have but as the platform for building something better than we've ever known. This marks the kind of commitment and vision that will see parents lift their parenting to new heights as well as pastors lead their congregations to new levels of effectiveness;

same Gospel and Word of God, new packages and structures of relevance to the world.

CHAPTER SUMMARY

Transformational leaders place high value on creating a culture of innovation. They know that creativity is core to the success and stability of the organization, and they build innovation into the fabric of the family or organization by encouraging ownership (urging team members to act as though they had an ownership stake), taking risks, and allowing for failure. All of this happens while holding steadfastly and consistently to a strong moral compass, and creating very open communication channels. None of these steps come easily or naturally, but with intentionality and discipline they release significant creativity.

SOME POSSIBLE EXERCISES

Encourage Ownership

Ask five or six people whom you know in your church, club, or workplace, "If you were in charge, what changes would you make to this place? And why?" Listen. Take notes. Don't get defensive. What did you hear that might be worth consideration?

Take Risks

Would you describe yourself as a risk-taker? If not, what holds you back? How risk-averse are you? Find two people in your circles who rates themselves above average on a risk scale. Have a conversation with them. Probe as deeply as possible. Where do they get their courage and confidence?

Allow for Failure

How do you speak to your spouse, children, or family when they fail at something? Do you react strongly with open criticism? Or more subtly with gentle, shaming digs? If you respond in either of these ways, practice different (supportive and encouraging) ways to "allow for failure." Then use what you have practiced, to minimize your own critical spirit.

NOTES

Key thoughts you had while reading this chapter. **Questions** that came up. **Ideas** for personal next steps. **Insights** to discuss with a friend.

_____

_____

_____

_____

_____

_____

Close

In the preceding chapters, many leadership topics have remained relatively untouched. What about resilience in leadership? Conflict management? The inner life and spiritual life of the leader? Financial literacy? Communication skills? Ongoing professional development? These and many other legitimate questions and concerns deserve our careful attention. However, transformational leadership — the most comprehensive single model for leadership of the last fifty years — provides a rich and powerful foundation upon which these other matters build.

Leadership coaches abound, but so often they focus on technical challenges, broken communication channels, or inadequate organizational systems. This won't be enough.

Similarly, leadership articles and books are pouring forth, yet most lack a comprehensive model to frame the leadership conversation. On the one hand, often they shine a bright laser on a single facet of leadership — for example, effective negotiation skills, successful sales and marketing techniques, or better hiring practices. On the other hand, sometimes the authors fire a literary shotgun — blasting disparate pellets of information about everything imaginable — and hope that some of it sticks.

A philosophy of leadership — a simple, memorable, meaningful model — makes all the difference. It provides a structure upon which all else hangs. It creates a filter through which we can assess the validity and value of all else that we hear. That's what transformational leadership is all about.

TRANSFORMATIONAL LEADERSHIP
Producing change and building lives through authenticity, inspiration, empathy, and innovation.

This definition has guided our conversation from start to finish. We've not drilled excessively into each phrase or term. In fact, I've left plenty of room for you to add your own insights, and deepen this well for your own purposes and from your own resources. But transformational leadership does provide an anchor.

A boat in a storm may move up and down, even round and round, but if it has a firm anchor, it remains tethered within a reasonable field of movement. That's how I trust this book will function for you.

We've witnessed a significant shift in the field of leadership over the past four decades. Much of the material coming from secular sources in more recent times aligns remarkably well with Christian and biblical principles. The research consistently concludes that chemistry and character surpass competence in their importance, and the leadership literature repeatedly affirms the core principles of transformational leadership, often without realizing it.[116]

It's common to read books and articles that assume we all want to be Fortune 500 CEOs or change the world. Such vision is vastly too grandiose and inaccessible for most of us. We know that few of us will have the opportunity to influence governments, change global economic structures, or launch international movements of great consequence. However, it is entirely reasonable to believe that we can be women and men of deep influence in our homes, churches, communities, and businesses. I hope this book in some way has nurtured that vision within you and outlined a framework for greater effectiveness.

Where to from here?

The basic tenets of transformational leadership are not complicated. We produce change (for the common good) as we build lives (that flourish), and we do so with a consistent and untiring commitment to authenticity, inspiration, empathy, and innovation.

If you have not already been reading this book with a friend, another parent, or a work colleague, I'd suggest that you take one of these six "categories" (whichever strikes you as most timely and relevant) and begin to explore it more deeply. Try one or more of the suggested exercises at the end of the chapter, or build some of your own. Make some notes about what happens; how you felt and how others seemed to respond. Talk about it. Make sticky note reminders about it. Journal about it. Make it part of your daily language.

Language functions in two ways. It *reveals* how we think, but it also *forms* how we think. If we want to change our thinking (and therefore our actions and our outcomes) we must first change our language. That's why the talking, the writing, and the practicing matters. It builds transformational leadership "muscle memory."

You don't need to work systematically through each chapter in order. Each pillar both stands alone and functions interdependently with the others. Start where you feel most curious or compelled. But share the journey with someone else.

If all of us grasped the vision to be transformational leaders wherever we live, work, and serve then our collective efforts would indeed create a wave of strategic change. As always, it boils down to blooming where we are planted. So, let's not settle for mediocrity or just "more of the same." Let's look beyond profiteering or resume-building, past the traditional ideas of success and status, and begin to embrace more wholeheartedly the commitment to produce change and build lives through authenticity, inspiration, empathy, and innovation. We can only imagine what a collective commitment to this kind of leadership might yield, undergirded by faith in God and partnership with Christ.

ENDNOTES

Introduction

[1] Cohn, Jeffery & Jay Moran. (2011) *Why are We Bad at Picking Good Leaders?* San Francisco, CA: Jossey-Bass, p.4.

[2] See Lee Cowan's article: http://www.cbsnews.com/news/testing-a-universal-basic-income-stockton-california-economic-security-project. Accessed April 15, 2018.

[3] For additional background to Jonathan Edwards, see http://www.britannica.com, http://www.encyclopedia.com, and http://en.wikipedia.org.

[4] http://www.susan-pellowe.com.

[5] In the 1840s, famous historian Thomas Carlyle proposed that "the history of the world is but the biography of great men." His Great Man Theory of leadership taught that these great men were not the product of their society or their learning, but the ideal combination of godly motivation and personality.

[6] Allender, D. B. (2006) *Leading with a Limp: Turning your Struggles into Strengths.* Colorado Springs, CO: Waterbrook Press, p.27.

[7] Gladwell, M. (2015) *Blink: The Power of Thinking Without Thinking.* New York, NY: Back Bay Books, p.87.

[8] Gladwell, p.88.

[9] Hewlett, S.A. (2014) *Executive Presence.* New York, NY: Harper Collins, p.89.

[10] A 2017 Sherpa Executive Coaching Survey found that 60 percent of Executive Coaches charge over $300 per hour and 38 percent of Business Coaches do the same. Furthermore, the most recent seven-year trend indicates an increasing demand for qualified coaches, with insufficient coaches available to keep pace with that demand. http://www.sherpacoaching.com/pdf%20files/2017_Executive_Coaching_Survey_PUBLIC.pdf.

[11] As quoted in Gaddie, R.K. (2003) *Born to Run: Origins of the Political Career,* Lanham, MD: Rowman & Littlefield, p.119.

[12] Macintyre, B. (2017) *Rogue Heroes: The History of the SAS, Britain's Secret Special Forces Unit that Sabotaged the Nazis and Changed the Nature of War.* New York, NY: Broadway Books.

Chapter 1 — Transformational Leadership

[13] Google was founded in 1998 by Larry Page and Sergey Brin while they were PhD students at Stanford University, California. It's remarkable that Google has become so globally ubiquitous in such a short time. The name Google, however, did not emerge from Larry Page's reading. The name originated from a misspelling of the word "googol," the number 1 followed by 100 zeros, which was picked to signify that the search engine was intended to provide large quantities of information.

[14] Harnish, V. (2015) *Scaling up: How a Few Companies Make it, and Why the Rest Don't*. Ashburn, VA: Gazelles Inc., p.2.

[15] Sample, S. B. (2003) *The Contrarian's Guide to Leadership*. San Francisco, CA: Jossey-Bass.

[16] Some leadership scholars suggest that leadership is never the leader but the collaboration of all the parts that constitute movement. They delineate between leaders and leadership; one is a limited function while the other is a comprehensive process. My colleague, Dr. Dennis Nichols, draws this distinction very nicely.

[17] See http://quodid.com/quotes/8114/casey-stengel/the-key-to-being-a-good-manager-is

[18] A February 22, 2017 article on www.Forbes.com noted that "of all the reasons people leave companies, having a bad manager tops the list. According to Gallup polls, a full 50 percent of employees who quit cite their managers as the reason. People might join a company for the compensation, growth opportunities, or mission, but they frequently leave because they don't want to work for their manager any longer."

[19] Greenleaf, R. (1977) *The Power of Servant Leadership*. Oakland, CA: Berrett-Koehler Publishers.

[20] http://www.regent.edu/acad/global/publications/jvl/vol1_iss1/Spears_Final.pdf.

[21] Sipe, J. W., & Frick, D. M. (2009) *Seven Pillars of Servant Leadership: Practicing the Wisdom of Leading by Serving*. Mahwah, NJ: Paulist Press.

[22] Keith, K. 2nd ed. (2015) *The Case for Servant Leadership*. Atlanta, GA: The Greenleaf Center.

[23] In 1964, the last year of the baby boom, there were nearly 72.5 million baby boomers in the United States. This number rose to 78.8

million by 1999, including people who immigrated to the United States and were born between 1946 and 1964.

[24] See a full infographic at http://www.infoprolearning.com/blog/13-shocking-leadership-development-statistics-infopro-learning/.

Chapter 2 — Producing Change

[25] Cashman, K. Large print ed. (2010) *Leadership from the Inside Out*. San Francisco, CA: Berrett-Koehler Publishers, p.127. Science has found that, on average, 98 percent of the body's atoms are replaced every year (mostly through air, food, and liquid that we ingest) and that the body's cells undergo a thorough replacement every 7-10 years. See https://science.howstuffworks.com/life/cellular-micro scopic/does-body-really-replace-seven-years1.htm.

[26] Kotter, John P. (2012) *Leading Change*. Boston, MA: Harvard Business Press, p.33.

[27] See the helpful book by Kegan, R. & Lahey, L. (2009) *Immunity to Change: How to Overcome It and Unlock Potential in Yourself and Your Organization*. Boston, MA: Harvard Business Press.

[28] Kegan & Lahey, p.1.

[29] Kegan & Lahey, p.37.

[30] Kegan and Lahey (p.64) discuss these three dimensions of immunity to change. They also propose a powerful question for all leaders to ask of their peers and teams: *"What is the one big thing I need to do better?"* This can provide some great feedback for personal leadership development.

[31] The only exceptions to this are moments of crisis, where time is of the essence and failure to change will be immediately catastrophic. But most of us face very few such urgent moments in our leadership.

[32] Harnish, p.138.

[33] For example, the *Association of Theological Schools*, which accredits over 270 seminaries and graduate schools in Canada and North America, resisted approving fully-online degree programs until well after the for-profit educational market had seized the reins. Innovative seminaries found themselves hamstrung by accrediting bodies — and often still do.

[34] Brad Cunningham has written an excellent article on digital natives and digital immigrants, particularly as it helps faculty

understand students in higher education. See Cunningham, B. (2007) *Digital Native or Digital Immigrant, Which Language Do You Speak?* http://www.nacada.ksu.edu/Clearinghouse/AdvisingIssues/Digital-Natives.htm.

[35] See Colossians 3:8, 12. We find exhortations to change our thinking or behavior on virtually every page of the New Testament. For a dramatic sequence of this kind of ethical exhortation, see also Romans 12.

Chapter 3 — Building Lives

[36] Sinek, S. (2017) *Leaders Eat Last*. New York, NY: Penguin Group, p.21.

[37] Eugene Peterson speaks helpfully about this in *The Contemplative Pastor* (1993) Grand Rapids, MI: Eerdmans, pp.56-65. He notes multiple contrasts between "running the church" and "the cure of souls." Running the church seizes the initiative, takes control, motivates, and problem solves. The cure of souls assumes the initiative is with God, and is attentive and responsive to the work of God within others and what he is doing. In essence, it's the distinction (at times) between working *for* God and working *with* God.

[38] https://jessupleadership.com/2018/02/27/the-end-of-poverty/.

[39] Johann Hari's TED Talk is less about what addicts should do, and much more about how society might best support addicts. http://www.ted.com/talks/johann_hari_everything_you_think_you_know_about_addiction_is_wrong.

[40] Grant, Adam. (2013) *Give and Take*. New York, NY: Penguin Books, pp.6-7. By the end of his book, Grant divides givers into two groups and identifies the successful givers as "otherish." "By giving in ways that are energizing rather than exhausting, otherish givers are more likely to rise to the top" (p.185).

[41] See http://www.brainyquote.com/quotes/ralph_nader_110188.

[42] Lencioni, Patrick. (2002) *The Five Dysfunctions of a Team*. San Francisco, CA: Jossey-Bass.

[43] Lencioni, pp.187-189.

[44] Randall O'Brien in David Dockery, ed. (2011) *Christian Leadership Essentials*. Nashville, TN: B&H Publishing, p.301.

[45] Harnish, p.28.

Chapter 4 — Authenticity

[46] For additional details to this surprising experiment story, see www.architecturaldigest.com/story/the-shed-at-dulwich.

[47] www.andersen.sdu.dk.

[48] Harvard Business Review Press, 2015.

[49] Palmer, Parker. (1983) *To Know as We are Known*. New York, NY: Harper Collins, pp.44-45.

[50] Hewlett, pp.154, 156.

[51] Psychologists at Harvard and other universities have recognized the power of hidden (also called automatic, unconscious, or implicit biases) and developed excellent tests that can help leaders become more self-aware in this area. See, for example, http://www.tolerance.org/professional-development/test-yourself-for-hidden-bias.

[52] Gergen, D. (2000) *Eyewitness to Power: The Essence of Leadership: Nixon to Clinton*. New York, NY: Touchstone, p.346.

[53] As cited in Cohn and Moran, p.25.

[54] Kouzes, J.M. & B.Z. Posner. (2007) *The Leadership Challenge*, 4th ed. San Francisco, CA: Jossey-Bass.

[55] Sinek, p.187.

[56] Machiavelli, Niccolo. (2003) *The Prince*. New York, NY: Bantam Classic, p.66.

[57] One of the deep truths about sin is that it may be private but it is never strictly personal. What we do in private always leaks into our public life; into our relationships. If I am brooding over a wound or an offense and letting the root of bitterness form in me, it will eventually become an unintended poison to those around me, even if they don't fully understand what's going on. In leadership, if I am privately critical of my team or those I lead, it inevitably shapes my conversations and my interactions with those team-members. As I completed my undergraduate education, an old college professor of mine gave a piece of advice that has stuck with me for decades: "You cannot minister to those of whom you are critical." We might slightly modify those words without changing their accuracy: "You cannot *lead* those of whom you are critical." This does not preclude us from criticizing performance at times, but when we become critical of the person, assigning false motives to them, doubting their integrity,

suspicious of their intentions, or frustrated by their work ethic—particularly behind their back—it will be difficult to successfully lead them. This is also true of parenting.

[58] See Andre Lavoie's insightful blog post (April 28, 2015): "4 Reasons You Need to Embrace Transparency in the Workplace." http://www.entrepreneur.com/article/245461.

[59] See https://inside.unbounce.com/.

[60] https://blog.hubspot.com/blog/tabid/6307/bid/34234/the-hubspot-culture-code-creating-a-company-we-love.aspx

[61] https://americanaddictioncenters.org/rehab-guide/12-step/

[62] Longman, Karen A. ed. (2012) *Thriving in Leadership*. Abilene, TX: Abilene Press, pp.263-264.

[63] For more information, see the helpful summary article at http://www.mindtools.com/pages/article/level-5-leadership.htm.

[64] Timms, D. (2011) "Humility - No Options." *The Lookout*.

[65] Allender, pp.69-70.

Chapter 5 — Inspiration

[66] Gardner, H. (1995) *Leading Minds: An Anatomy of Leadership*. New York, NY: Basic Books, p.9.

[67] Pythagoras' Theorem: "In a right angled triangle: the square of the hypotenuse is equal to the sum of the squares of the other two sides."

[68] Kotter, p.9.

[69] http://www.cnbc.com/2015/02/04/money-is-the-leading-ca use-of-stress-in-relationships.html.

[70] http://www.pnas.org/content/107/38/16489.

[71] http://money.cnn.com/2018/05/29/news/economy/chick-fil -a-sacramento-wage/index.html.

[72] Kouzes, James & Barry Posner. (2004) *Christian Reflections on the Leadership Challenge*. San Francisco, CA: Jossey-Bass, pp. 34-36.

[73] Kotter, p.127.

[74] In Matthew's gospel we read this phrase 31 times. Quite prolific use!

Chapter 6 — Empathy

[75] Quoted by Pastor Curt Harlow, Bayside Adventure Church, Sunday February 11, 2018, Roseville, CA.

[76] Some studies estimate that one in five (or more) Americans will have some form of mental illness in their lifetime. https://adaa.org/about-adaa/press-room/facts-statistics

[77] Brown, Brené. (2010) *"The Power of Vulnerability."* TED Talk. http://www.ted.com/talks/Brené_brown_on_vulnerability?language=en.

[78] Kelley, David & Tom. (2013) *Creative Confidence.* New York, NY: Crown Publishing, p.74. This advice to empathize with the end-user has become increasingly well-understood and common. Donald Miller (www.storybrand.com) reminds people that in marketing "We are not the hero but the guide." His first observation? "Be empathetic. Customers are on a journey and have run into a problem. State it, and care."

[79] Kelley, pp.13-17.

[80] Sinek, p.9.

[81] Sample, p.21.

[82] Sample, p.29.

[83] Patterson, K., J. Grenny, R. McMillan, & A. Switzler. 2nd ed. (2012) *Crucial Conversations: Tools for Talking When Stakes are High.* New York, NY: McGraw Hill, p.53.

[84] Patterson, et al., pp.58-61. The authors then propose that we create safe environments by implementing the following steps: 1) Commit to seek mutual purpose; 2) Recognize the purpose behind the strategy; 3) Invent a mutual purpose; and 4) Brainstorm new strategies (pp.90-98).

[85] Mark Goulston (*Just Listen*, AMACOM, 2015) was an FBI hostage negotiator who taught people how to de-escalate tense situations by building empathy. He suggested three tips to better empathize with others: First, pay attention to body language. Crossed arms, angry expressions, or rigid shoulders, tell us something. If you spot someone like this, do not try to get through with facts or reason. Just give them plenty of room to express whatever they need to say. Do not interrupt. Second, don't take issue with anything they say. Resist defensiveness. Finally, after all is said, don't jump to talk. This shuts down people. Instead, after they pause, simply say, "Tell me more." People in pain rarely feel heard. Asking for more allows deeper healing to occur.

[86] http://www.stephencovey.com/7habits/7habits-habit5.php. Note that in Denmark, school children have a weekly hour called Klassen Time, when students come together to discuss problems and

help each other. They do this from age six until they graduate from high school. Sheryl Sandberg (2017) writes: "The children learn empathy by hearing others' perspectives and reflecting on how their behavior affects those around them" (*Option B: Facing Adversity, Building Resilience, and Finding Joy.* New York, NY: Alfred A. Knopf, p.116).

[87] Bonhoeffer, Dietrich. *Letters and Papers from Prison.* New York, NY: Touchstone Books, 1997. Bonhoeffer wrote this quote about empathy while he sat in prison awaiting the hangman's noose which came in 1945. His notes were first published in 1951.

[88] Cohn and Moran (p.69) ask: "What does it mean to say that a leader possesses emotional intelligence? The answers lie in three questions: 1. Do I know myself? 2. Can I control myself? 3. Do I look for ways to improve?"

[89] Grant, Adam. (2016) *Originals: How Non-Conformists Move the World.* New York, NY: Penguin Books, p.9.

[90] For a brief analysis of these oft-cited statistics, see http://www.nonverbalgroup.com/2011/08/how-much-of-communication-is-really-nonverbal.

[91] This statement is commonly attributed first to William Temple (1881-1944), the 98th Archbishop of Canterbury (1942-1944).

[92] Brown, Brené. (2010) *"The Power of Vulnerability."* TED Talk. http://www.ted.com/talks/brene_brown_on_vulnerability.

[93] It has become increasingly common for businesses to identify more than one "bottom line" (financial profit) in business. The double-bottom line principle speaks to the financial profit of a company but also the greater social good that it produces. The triple-bottom line adds environmental consciousness (and sustainable practices) to the responsibilities of the company. Indeed, some scholars are now writing about the quadruple-bottom line which incorporates the three elements noted above *plus* the obligation to pursue the transformation (often spiritual) of their customers.

[94] http://abcnews.go.com/Business/story?id=5503956&page=1. Interestingly, Oxfam urged Nike not to close the factory but to simply rectify the abuses that workers had experienced. See http://www.oxfam.org.au/2008/07/forced-labour-by-nike-supplier.

[95] See http://www.newsweek.com/florida-shooting-survivor-trump-call-818443.

[96] See http://www.businessinsider.com/parkland-shooting-survivor-reacts-to-her-phone-call-with-donald-trump-2018-2.

[97] Catmull, Ed. (2014) *Creativity, Inc.* New York, NY: Random House, p.73

[98] R. Judson Carlberg in David Dockery, ed. (2011) *Christian Leadership Essentials*. Nashville, TN: B&H Publishing, p.91.

Chapter 7 — Innovation

[99] See Sir Ken Robinson's compelling critique in his 2006 TED Talk which has been viewed well over 50 million times, http://www.ted.com/talks/ken_robinson_says_schools_kill_creativity.

[100] The inspiring story of Richard Montanez can be found at http://www.foodbeast.com/news/a-humble-mexican-janitor-accidentally-invented-flamin-hot-cheetos-and-this-is-his-life/.

[101] Allender, p.68.

[102] See Yoram Solomon's analysis (and rejection) of this practice at www.inc.com/yoram-solomon/20-of-my-time-will-not-make-me-more-creative. Solomon asserts that time given to employees for creativity will ultimately be used for other purposes because creativity is rarely turned on and off with the clock.

[103] See https://online.sbu.edu/news/2016/06/28/where-kodak-failed-and-netflix-didnt-lesson-innovation. The article provides a fascinating contrast between the decline of Kodak and the rise of Netflix.

[104] Scott Anthony's insightful Harvard Business Review article (July 15, 2016) argued that Kodak failed at many levels, but ultimately at not correctly anticipating the disruptive innovation of the film and photo industry. https://hbr.org/2016/07/kodaks-downfall-wasnt-about-technology.

[105] http://www.brainyquote.com/quotes/michael_jordan_127660.

[106] In 2010, Peter Madsen and Vinit Desai researched what factors predict whether or not a space flight will succeed. They tracked every space flight launch for nearly 50 years, by nearly 30 organizations (government and private), and found that from the more than 4,000 launches, the more times a government failed to put a rocket into orbit successfully, the more likely they were to succeed on the next try; and the greater the failure — a major explosion, for example — the higher their chances of success the next time. See "Failing to Learn? The Effects of Failure and Success on

Organizational Learning in the Global Orbital Launch Vehicle Industry." *Academy of Management Journal* 53 (2010): 451-476.

[107] Kelley, p.43.

[108] See also Brené Brown in her TED Talk, "*Listening to Shame*" (March 2012) in which she explains that failing to meet the standard of perfection often contributes to women feeling shame. Thus, we get trapped in a vicious cycle of feeling shame after missing the perfectionist mark and then maintaining shame because our imperfections make us too afraid to express the authenticity that turns shame away. It's a no-win situation. Hear the full talk at http://www.ted.com/talks/Brene_brown_listening_to_shame?language=em.

[109] Hiller, Ann. "It's Not About Perfection." *Popular Woodworking Magazine*, April 2018, #238: 64

[110] Of course, it's one thing to accept the failure of others but quite another matter to handle *our own failure* well. Psychologist Martin Seligman has identified three P's that can stunt our recovery from loss and undercut our resilience as leaders. These P's sometimes come into play when we experience trauma or loss. Grief opens the door to these soul-sapping P's. But these P's also threaten leaders who experience failure or setback. **Personalization:** The belief that we are wholly and solely to blame for a failure or setback. *"It's all my fault; it wouldn't have happened if I had been more attentive, more present, more intuitive, more something."* **Pervasiveness:** The belief that a particular failure will affect all areas of our lives and ruin everything. *"This ruins everything; my relationships, my reputation, my family, my finances."* **Permanence:** The belief that a failure or setback will last forever. *"I'll never recover; I'll feel this way till the day I die."* In her compelling book on facing adversity, building resilience, and finding joy, Sheryl Sandberg (*Option B*, p.16) notes that "Hundreds of studies have shown that children and adults recover more quickly when they realize that hardships aren't entirely their fault, don't affect every aspect of their lives, and won't follow them everywhere forever."

[111] Cashman, pp.77-78.

[112] See http://www.investopedia.com/terms/v/venturecapitalist.asp. Kevin Cashman (*Leadership from the Inside Out*: 149) notes that "According to the Hoover Institute, 66 percent of venture capital start-ups fail to return the original investment."

[113] Wagner, T. & T Dintersmith. (2015) *Most Likely To Succeed*. New York, NY: Scribner Press, p.25

[114] Catmull, p.64.

[115] http://www.tesla.com/blog/all-our-patent-are-belong-you.

Close

[116] Cohn and Moran's book *Why are We Bad at Picking Good Leaders* (San Francisco, CA: Jossey-Bass, 2011), provides confirmation of the key elements in this book. After twenty years of mentoring large companies and their CEOs, the authors concluded that the core indicators for likely leadership success are not charisma and energy but integrity, empathy, emotional intelligence, vision, judgment, courage, and passion. Their conclusions align remarkably closely with the chapters and content within this book.

Made in the USA
San Bernardino, CA
28 April 2019